Winning Bedtime Battles

WINNING BEDTIME BATTLES

Getting Your Children (Ages 2–10) to Sleep

Charles E. Schaefer, Ph.D. and
Theresa Foy DiGeronimo, M. Ed.

A Citadel Press Book
Published by Carol Publishing Group

Dedication

To my Karine whose early nighttime adventures prompted me to study childhood sleep problems.

C.S.

To my Joey—the world's most persistent bedtime battler.

T.D.

Carol Publishing Group Edition, 1995

A Citadel Press Book
Published by Carol Publishing Group
Citadel Press is a registered trademark of Carol Communications, Inc.

Editorial Offices: 600 Madison Avenue, New York, NY 10022
Sales & Distribution Offices: 120 Enterprise Avenue, Secaucus, NJ 07094
In Canada: Canadian Manda Group, One Atlantic Avenue, Suite 105
Toronto, Ontario, M6K 3E7

Queries regarding rights and permissions should be addressed to:
Carol Publishing Group, 600 Madison Avenue, New York, NY 10022

Manufactured in the United States of America
15 14 13 12 11 10 9 8 7 6 5 4 3 2

Carol Publishing Group books are available at special discounts
for bulk purchases, sales promotions, fund raising, or
educational purposes. Special editions can also be created to
specifications. For details contact: Special Sales Department,
Carol Publishing Group, 120 Enterprise Ave., Secaucus, NJ 07094

Library of Congress Cataloging-in-Publication Data

Schaefer, Charles E.
        Winning bedtime battles / by Charles E. Schaefer and Theresa Foy
    DiGeronimo.
            p. cm.
    "A Citadel Press book."
    ISBN 0-8065-1318-7 (paper)
        1. Children—Sleep. 2. Sleep disorders in children. 3. Children-
    Care. I. DiGeronimo, Theresa Foy. II. Title.
RJ506.S55S34   1992   91-46785
618.92'8498—dc20   CIP

Contents

Preface

In my clinical practice at Fairleigh Dickinson University in New Jersey, I specialize in helping families recognize and remedy children's sleep problems. Now, through the pages of this book, I hope to do the same for you. As I explain to the parents who come to the clinic, before you can solve the problem you'll need to find the cause of the nighttime dilemma. With this in mind, the book has been organized in three parts to help you quickly determine why your children won't go to sleep easily with a simple kiss and a smile. The introduction to each part gives you an overview of possible causes from which you can pick the most likely culprit in your child's case. Once you've decided on the probable cause, you can use the suggested strategies in that chapter to solve the problem and foster healthy sleep habits that will last a lifetime.

In many of our homes the time between when we announce "It's time for bed" and the time when our children actually fall asleep is one of great struggle. So Part One, "Bedtime Resistance," focuses on the reasons and the solutions for the bedtime difficulties that mark the end of each day with crying, yelling, and full-blown tantrums. This section also examines how and why the bedtime hour is often stretched toward midnight with delaying, stalling, and ignoring tactics. And finally (and sometimes most importantly to fatigued parents who've already fought the going-to-bed battle), Part One explains the reasons why children who wake in the middle of the night and call to their parents or climb into their beds need to be taught how to sleep through the night.

Although the majority of bedtime battles are caused by children's reluctance to call it a day, the problem often lies in childhood fears. Part Two, "Bedtime Fears," takes a close look at children who resist bedtime because they are genuinely afraid of the night. This section details the causes and cures for fears of the dark, night monsters, separation, and nightmares. It will also help you decide if your child's bedtime problems are caused by these fears or by bad habits like those described in Part One. I know it can be difficult to distinguish the "I'm afraid" cries of a truly fearful child from the same cries delivered by a bedtime manipulator, but the information in these chapters will give you the facts you need to recognize the difference.

Finally, I've included in Part Three, "Bedtime Problems," a discussion of less common but equally worrisome circumstances that cause bedtime crying and misunderstandings. Sleepwalking and night terrors are sleep disturbances that cause parents, more than the affected children, great concern and upset. So, to keep these nighttime occurrences from turning unnecessarily into traumatic experiences, the third section gives you detailed information about the cause, treatment, and prevention of these enigmas. Part Three also discusses some disorders that can result in sleep problems sometimes mistakenly thought to be caused by general resistance. Knowing how insomnia, apnea, and narcolepsy can affect sleep patterns and daily functioning will help you know when your children need medical help rather than discipline or psychological counseling.

I have found that almost all cases of bedtime battles fought by children between the ages of two and ten can be resolved with the knowledge and strategies I've gathered together in this book. But occasionally a child's sleep problems are so intense and stubborn that professional help is needed to overcome them. If your child still battles against you, night fears, or fatigue even after you've determined the reason for his or her poor sleep habits and have incorporated the suggested nighttime tactics into your child's bedtime routine, then check the information in the Epilogue. It will tell you how to decide if your child needs professional help and, if so, how to get it.

Bedtime should mark the peaceful time at the end of each day when parents and children express their feelings of love and affection for each other and share their hopes and dreams for happy tomorrows. Unfortunately, in many households the way the day *should* end and the way it *does* end are quite different scenerios. If your nights are filled with tantrums, fears, or worries, then this book is for you. It has been written to help you better understand why children behave the way they do at night and how you can regain the good night's sleep you both need and deserve.

Acknowledgments

We would like to thank our agent, Faith Hamlin, who always knows how to get a good idea into print.

PART I
Bedtime Resistance

In the ideal world of parent/child relationships, parents are all-loving and all-in-charge, children are all-loving and all-obedient, and bedtime means no more than the blissful end of another day. In this perfect world, the parent says, "Come on, Johnny, it's time for bed." And Johnny jumps up, heads toward the bedroom saying, "Okay, good night. I'll see you in the morning."

In the real world, however, bedtime is more likely to be a battle of wills between parent and child. Calls of, "Time for bed, Johnny," are answered with strategic tactics that range from screams of protest to blatant ignoring. The battle to stay up past the announced bedtime and to wander out of bed during the night drags on until the person with the most persistence and stamina finally wins. Not surprisingly, it is children who invariably have a greater supply of these two tide-swaying characteristics. Finally (it sometimes takes years of on-again-off-again fighting), parents surrender—bedtime then becomes whenever and where ever the children choose.

News and magazine articles have reported changing attitudes toward an established bedtime. A recent *New York Times* article states, "In many American households, a child's bedtime has become a flexible matter. While parents remember being sent to bed at seven P.M., their children are going to sleep at nine, ten, or even eleven at night."[1] You may recognize similar changes in your own family, but like many other parents, you may have come to a

1

point in the bedtime conflict where you've decided to overlook the fact that your children have no set bedtime hour. This usually happens when you run out of ammunition (hollering, bribery, and threats eventually lose their impact), and your energy supply at the end of each day is painfully depleted. If you have reached this point, don't despair—the fact that you're reading this book says that you haven't yet lost on the bedtime front. In the following chapters, you'll find all you need to turn that little bit of hope into unbeatable resolve. Read on!

WHY BOTHER?

To take the first step toward finding a resolution to bedtime battles, you need to determine for yourself that an appropriate bedtime is necessary to your child's health and well-being. Consider these facts: It is during sleep that a child's body renews its energy supply and restores its biological rhythms. Lack of sleep can cause children to feel disoriented and "off" during the day. Physical problems such as headaches, body tension, fatigue, and a variety of other nonspecific aches and pains also can be the result of lack of sleep.

How long and how soundly your child sleeps affects not only physical health, but also daily moods and behavior patterns. The child who teeters on the edge of fatigue each day is bound to be sluggish, grumpy, and prone to emotional outburst. He or she may also lack motivation and develop a low frustration level.

School performance, too, is directly tied into sleep patterns. Insufficient sleep reduces academic accomplishments in several ways. It impairs the short-term memory and so tired students display greater difficulty in performing tasks that require recall of facts or transference of information. Sleep loss also negatively affects one's ability to concentrate, thus weary children are more likely to spend class time daydreaming, losing track of their work, or feeling frustrated at their inability to pay attention. Also, problem-solving situations become especially difficult for sleep-deprived children because their decision-making skills are notably affected by fatigue.

You should feel justified (and not guilty) in setting an appropriate bedtime hour because you need and deserve time for yourself and your spouse. Between your child's bedtime and your own is perhaps the only time you have to do things for yourself each day. You need time to read, relax, call a friend, and certainly focus on your marriage. Children who stay up far past a reasonable bedtime rob their parents of private time which serves to restore the parents' emotional strength and sanity.

And lastly, you should feel that a noncombative bedtime atmosphere is something worth striving for. In my clinical practice, I have found that when children and their parents end each day in angry power plays, everyone feels defeated; these feelings often spill over into negative daytime attitudes and behaviors. Because bedtime battles have such far-reaching effects on the parent/child relationship, assure yourself that by trying to establish a reasonable routine you're not following a mere whim that says it might be nice if your children went off without complaint at a set bedtime. Determine that your efforts are aimed at what's right and best for the healthy and peaceful functioning of your family. Once you've given yourself this positive mindset, you'll be better equipped to withstand the barrage of objections that your children may initially use as return fire.

Although some bedtime problems are caused by emotional and psychological difficulties (as explained in Part Two), the vast majority of children resist going to bed simply because they prefer to stay awake. They worry that wonderful things will happen when they fall asleep. They imagine they'll miss something exciting, or even worse—a TV show. The solution to this most common bedtime problem is found in an easy-to-establish discipline strategy that is spelled out in advance and is consistently enforced. In the following four chapters I've mapped out a disciplinary approach that is tailored to counter the battle cries of children who (1) would rather not go to bed, (2) stubbornly refuse to go to bed without full-blown tantrums, (3) stall and delay going to sleep with requests for "one more" drink, kiss, and trip to the toilet, and (4) go to bed, but then keep popping back up.

CHAPTER 1

Bad Bedtime Habits

"**S**even P.M.: We announce, 'Robert, it's time to get ready for bed.'

7:04, 7:09, 7:12, 7:14, 7:17, 7:18, 7:22, 7:24, 7:25, 7:26, 7:27: We announce to Robert that he really has to start getting ready for bed Right Now and we are Not Kidding."

This excerpt from *Dave Barry's Guide to Marriage and/or Sex* illustrates how bedtime typically begins in households all over America. Barry goes on to note how at 7:43 Robert begins taking off his clothes and putting on his pajamas, and how at 9:27 Robert has removed his shirt and one shoe. The tale continues to chronicle Robert's wash-up regime, sudden need for food, rebrushing of teeth, and a final bedtime story that brings the family to:

"10:43, 10:47, 10:51, 10:54, 10:56, and 10:59: We announce that it really is time to go to bed Right Now and we are Not Kidding."[2]

This tale strikes us as funny because it touches on something so common—the out-of-control bedtime regimen. It may be funny in print, but we all know it's not funny when it happens in our homes.

WHY KIDS ARE ALLOWED TO STAY UP LATE

When we know for certain that children need a good night's

sleep, why are so many allowed to stay up late? I believe it happens because, for a variety of reasons, we, parents, have difficulty establishing and enforcing a set bedtime hour.

For example:

Reason 1: Too Tired

Thirty-four-year-old Marge Heally says she's just too tired to enforce the eight o'clock bedtime rule she feels would be best for her kids. "I don't have enough energy to argue all night. My three kids win every time: one whines, the other cries, and the third just ignores me. By the time I get the last one tucked in—the first one pops up again. I've given up trying. Now, whenever they're tired enough, they fall asleep."

Reason 2: Too Guilty

Twenty-seven-year-old Roger usually works late, and his four-year-old son likes to wait up for him. "We let Kenny stay up until I get home," Roger explains, "because if he goes to bed at eight-thirty I'd barely have time to say 'Hello' to him. We know he should go to bed earlier, but my wife and I both work and we don't have the heart to argue with him; he goes to day-care all day and if we make him go to bed, we feel like we're pushing him aside again."

Reason 3: Too Distracted

Sometimes the evening hours slip away before anyone realizes that bedtime is long past. Real-estate broker Amy Schell admits, "By the time I get the dishes done, give Karen and Keri their baths, throw in the laundry, sort out the day's mail, and make a few business phone calls, the kids have fallen asleep watching TV. In my heart, I want to tuck each one into bed at a reasonable hour and read them a bedtime story, but life is just too busy sometimes."

Unfortunately, on the nights when Amy does have the time for tucking in, her children don't want any part of it. They like watching TV till they drop and they complain loudly if their mom tries to change that routine.

Reason 4: Too Permissive

Many children do not have a scheduled bedtime because their parents tend to be permissive disciplinarians. When single parent, Pat, says to her seven-year-old son, "Gary, it's time for bed," he automatically yells, "NO!" Pat never insists because Gary's used to having his own way and can carry a fight on longer than she can. "Gary's generally a good kid," Pat reasons. "If he doesn't want to go to bed, he doesn't have to. I don't make a big deal about that kind of stuff. I figure, when he's tired, he'll go to bed."

Reason 5: Too Protective

Jay wants his four-year-old daughter in bed at seven-thirty every night. Some nights Kelly quite obediently goes to bed with a smile and a big kiss for her daddy. But most nights she doesn't. "Three or four nights a week, Kelly will complain that she can't go to bed," explains Jay, "because (a) she's afraid of the dark, (b) there's a bad guy in her room, or (c) she's afraid of having a bad dream. I think she's making this stuff up just to stay up longer, but on the outside chance she really is afraid, I'd feel like an ogre if I insisted that she go to bed anyway. So, I let her fall asleep by me on the couch and then I carry her up to bed."

SOLUTIONS THAT DON'T WORK

I have seen so many parents give up enforcing bedtime limits because the solutions used to calm the arguing don't work. In fact, looking for ways to end the bedtime war, we sometimes create new problems. For example, parents of preschoolers, like Jay, can often calm screams of protest by offering to lie down next to their children, sit nearby, or sing or read to them until they fall asleep. This solves the immediate problem of resisting bedtime, but it creates two new ones. First, this "solution" steals personal time from the parent who has to stay with the child for as long as it takes for the child to fall asleep. Earlier I encouraged you to consider a variety of reasons for winning bedtime battles. In addition to the most obvious one which emphasizes the need to protect the child's health and well-being, a second, equally valid, reason is to safeguard your own mental health. Parental burnout is a very real consequence of never having time to yourself. Contributing to this problem, certainly, is the habit of "putting" your child to sleep, thus reducing the amount of personal time you can enjoy each day. (Exceptions to this rule warranted by genuine nighttime fears are explained in Part Two.)

Second, staying in the bedroom gives you the responsibility of "putting" the child to sleep. "Putting" to sleep is a bad habit which robs children of their innate ability to fall asleep by themselves. This habit often begins in infancy when parents find that their babies will fall asleep more readily under certain conditions. Some drift off quickly if they're rocked, walked, or patted on the back. Others get accustomed to carriage or even car rides. These techniques do put babies to sleep, but often turn them into nightcriers. Unlike self-soothers who wake during the night (as we all do), lie quiet and then fall back to sleep, babies who are accustomed to being put to sleep usually wake during the night and cry persistently until someone comes to reestablish the sleep aids they've been conditioned to need.

If you still put your child to sleep, not only do you lose time for yourself and teach your child bad sleep habits, but it is quite likely that you've created a nightwaker. Like night-crying infants, nightwakers disturb your sleep throughout the night; now that they are older they use excuses like, "I need a drink," "I heard a noise," or, "I want to sleep in your bed." This happens because when your child awakes, you're not there to lull him or her back to sleep. The problems of nightwakers are detailed in Chapter Four, but you can head off the problem and begin to plan effective strategies to overcome bedtime resistance by remembering that it's not your job to make your child fall asleep and so you have no responsibility to try.

You can more easily pull away from the ineffective, putting-to-sleep solution by clarifying for yourself the difference between your bedtime responsibilities and your child's. Sleep duties should be divided in this way:

YOUR JOB: Provide a consistent bedtime routine; get your child into bed at a predetermined time; establish an environment conducive to sleep (quiet, calm, darkened room), and prohibit arousing activities at bedtime such as TV, radio, videos, or active play.

YOUR CHILD'S JOB: Fall asleep.

Once you've made this distinction, you can begin to organize a routine that will foster peaceful bedtimes that do not require the time investment needed to put a child to sleep.

When children grow too old to have someone sit in their room until they fall asleep, some parents allow the TV to replace them as the party responsible for putting these kids to sleep. Judging by the large numbers of children who fall asleep at the tube, this is a seemingly effective and easy answer to the bedtime dilemma—but it is not a desirable one because it, too, creates more problems than it remedies. Most problematic in this solution is the obvious fact that if the night's TV programming is interesting enough, children will stay awake far past the time that is appropriate for their sleep needs. School administrators are well aware of this occurrence because with increasing frequency teachers are reporting that many of their youngest students can relate the details of late-night TV shows but then fall asleep in class.

Yelling is another method that parents of older children find quite effective in persuading them into bed. But this tactic works only in the immediate instance when forcefully and persistently applied. Children will not reason that they should go to bed on time today because Mom or Dad yelled yesterday. Consequently, you need to use the strategy often—this obviously won't promote the peaceful bedtime you've set as a goal.

SOLUTIONS THAT DO WORK

There are a number of preparatory strategies I recommend you consider before you move in to take back the night from your children. The following three strategies will show you how you can improve your chances of success by planning ahead to create a predictable bedtime routine and set an appropriate bedtime hour.

Create Bedtime Rituals

Pleasant bedtime rituals ease the transition from being awake to being asleep by helping children feel more secure and comfortable about what they can expect at the end of every day. As you prepare to change poor bedtime habits into positive ones, put together a predictable sequence of events that you can consistently follow in the same order every night. This might involve the process of putting on PJs, brushing teeth, and reading a goodnight story. Or, your ritual may involve a bath and a song, and a story, and another song, and a glass of water, and another story. It's up to you to decide if you want to make it quick and easy or if you want to allow twenty to thirty minutes for special and exclusive time with your child for reading, talking, and being together.

Whichever rituals you choose, make sure they are ones that you'll have the time and energy to repeat every night and that sitters can duplicate. On her first night back to work, Darla found out the hard way just how important a bedtime ritual is to her two-year-old son. Darla told her mother-in-law, who was baby-sitting, that Danny would go to bed without any problems at seven o'clock. When she returned home at nine, she was shocked to find Danny awake and crying and her mother-in-law looking exhausted. It seems that when Grandma scooped up Danny at seven, placed him in his crib and left the room, he couldn't go right to sleep (as his mother said he would) because he wasn't prepared. He had learned to anticipate bedtime through the ritual of having a snack, reading a story on his mom's lap, then hearing her sing a lullaby as she turned on the nightlight. Then his mom would cover him with his favorite blanket and whisper, "Good night." For Danny, and for children of all ages, predictable bedtime rituals give time to unwind and to anticipate sleep; they also often eliminate bedtime conflicts.

Rituals help children see bedtime as a happy, normal way to end the day. Be sure to perform most of your rituals (such as reading or singing) in the bedroom itself. Children should view their bedroom as a safe and pleasurable place—a haven for rest and comfort. If this is the place where they get your undivided attention at the end of the day, they will be more likely to see it in these positive ways and be more willing to go there. For this reason, don't punish your children during the day by sending them to their bedrooms. This contributes to the punitive associations that bedtime sometimes trigger in children.

Although many older children still love a bedtime story or a special nighttime talk with Mom and Dad, some prefer to create their own bedtime routine. Give these children at least fifteen minutes alone in their rooms to listen to music, read, or do anything that helps them quietly unwind. When time's up, go in and say, "Good night," and turn off the lights. If you give your children (whatever their ages) predictable schedules, they're more likely to give you a peaceful "Good night."

Set a Bedtime Hour
There is no absolutely correct bedtime hour. To find the one best for your child, you must first consider your child's age. Although we each have personally unique sleep requirements, experts generally agree that children up to two-and-a-half years of age need ten to thirteen hours of sleep each day, three-to-five-year-olds need ten to twelve hours, and six-to-ten-year-olds need at least ten hours of sleep each night. Although these figures are only averages, it is unlikely that our child's total daily sleep time will differ by several hours. In addition to this information, you should use your observations to determine an appropriate bedtime. On their present schedule, do your children have difficulty waking in the morning? Are they regularly irritable, fatigued, or overly active during the day? Do they fall asleep in the late afternoon or early evening? Do they sleep an extra hour or more on weekends? If you answer "Yes" to more than one of these questions, you should assume that your children need more sleep than they are currently getting.

After determining how much sleep your child needs, you should consider your daily schedule before setting a bedtime. Remember, you'll need to leave time for your bedtime rituals. If you want to set a bedtime of eight-thirty, for example, you'll need to begin the ritual well before then. You should also consider your morning schedule; if your children are not yet in school, you might set a late bedtime if they can (and will) sleep late in the morning. But if they must get up early to go to the baby-sitter, day-care center, or school, then you'll have to establish a bedtime hour that keeps this waking schedule in mind.

If you feel they are old enough (usually by the age of eight), you can consult your children for their opinion on an appropriate bedtime hour. Sit down for a family conference and explain your concerns about the present bedtime routine and your plans to establish a new one. State your proposal, ask their opinion, and leave room in your initial plan for compromise. If your children are avid TV watchers, take out the programming guide and see which shows can be viewed without a problem, which ones require negotiation and compromise, and which ones are off-limits. If you have a VCR, you can offer to record late shows for viewing the next day. If there is a special "can't-be-missed" show which airs a reasonably short time after the proposed bedtime, you might use that as an incentive. Tell your children, "If you go to bed at the given time without complaint each night this week, you can stay up to watch that show." (See Chapter Two for more details on offering rewards as incentives.) Whenever possible, let your children work with you to set the new bedtime routine. It is well documented, and in my own practice I have seen, that when children have a say in making the rules, they are much more likely to follow them.

Be sure to periodically review your scheduled bedtime hour because children's sleep needs change as they get older. You can sometimes avoid conflicts by checking the average sleep needs previously mentioned to be sure your child actually requires the number of sleep hours you insist on.

Be Consistent

Regardless of what hour you choose or what ritual you follow, the key to successfully establishing a peaceful bedtime lies in consistency. Once you've decided on a bedtime hour, stick to it. Children need firm limits that they can count on as absolute. If you set an eight o'clock bedtime, don't send them to bed at eight one night, 8:12 the next, and 8:30 the one after that. Make it eight o'clock on the dot every night. If you're wishy-washy in the face of protest, or if you give in too often, or if you are adamant one night and lackadaisical the next, you confuse your children and place them in an unpredictable environment. This situation, alone, can produce more rebellion and maximize children's chances of victory.

Bedtime in the Farrell house, for example is at eight P.M. for five-year-old Mike, and at 8:45 for ten-year-old Kathy. Most often Mike Sr. strictly enforces these curfews, but once in a while (maybe once or twice a week) he's too busy or too tired to get up and escort each child to bed on time, so he gives in to their pleas and lets them both go to bed at nine. "I've really had it with fighting every night," he says. "The only nights these kids get to bed on time are when I get angry, yell, and stand up and bring them to their rooms. I'm tired of saying 'Good night' by slamming the door." Because Mike gives in to their arguing once in awhile, his kids do it every night—there's no other way of knowing which night is a "lucky" one. Once Mike learned to consistently enforce the bedtime routine and his children realized they couldn't win anymore, they gave up trying to change his mind.

If one parent wants to enforce a bedtime routine, but the other doesn't, the children soon learn how to divide and conquer by playing one parent against the other until they get their own way. Unfortunately, the children ultimately win, with the parents left arguing in the background. Children get an unsettling dose of guilt and insecurity; in addition, the discipline structure of the household is weakened. For example, legal secretary Joan Peterson wants her three young children in bed at what she calls "a decent hour." "I don't have a chance of doing this though," she says. "Not only do I have to hear the complaints from the kids, but then my husband chimes in with his usual, 'Oh, leave them alone. They'll go to bed in a little while.' Sometimes I insist, but then everybody in the house is mad at me so most of the time I don't feel it's worth the hassle." Joan's probably right; until she and her husband agree that their children need a certain amount of sleep hours each night, she won't be able to win the bedtime war. In fact, Joan probably doesn't win any disciplinary confrontations if her children have learned to respond, "I'll ask Daddy.

He'll say, 'Yes.'" Before you attempt to break bad bedtime habits, make sure you and your spouse are consistently willing to enforce the new rules.

Consistency is a vital element in determining the success or failure of this approach. There, of course, will be nights when you can be a bit flexible. You might, for example, make an exception when an out-of-town relative stops in for a visit, or you might agree to set aside one weekend night for staying up a little later. As long as the exceptions don't become the rule, and the bedtime isn't stretched more than an hour, the sleep habits you're building won't be unduly sabotaged.

PUT YOUR PLAN INTO ACTION

Once you've set the stage for peaceful bedtimes by teaming up with your spouse and giving your children advance notice of the new routine, you're ready to put your plan into action. Every night, whenever possible, consistently observe the following four steps. At first the plan may not run smoothly because your children have been conditioned in the past to protest and then get their own way. It will take at least one week (and at most, one month) for them to learn to accept calmly the inevitability of bedtime.

Step One: Enforce Quiet Time

Reserve the hour before bedtime for quiet play. This will lower your children's activity level and prepare their nervous system for relaxation. Roughhousing, running, playing tickling games, and for some children watching certain TV shows, make peaceful transition to sleep especially difficult. Encourage reading, quiet board games, or music. (If you find that homework is a frustrating task for your child, try to have it completed before the quiet time.)

Step Two: Give Advance Notice

One-half hour before you want to begin your bedtime routine, give advance warning to your children. Announce: "A half hour till bedtime." This gives children the opportunity to mentally prepare for the switch from awake to sleep time and also to finish whatever activity they're engaged in. Then ten minutes before bedtime, give another warning. You might use some kind of timer to signal when the ten minutes are up; a kitchen timer, a stovetop buzzer, or even a clock radio will do. This allows an impersonal third party to announce bedtime. In any case, you should find the method that is most comfortable for you.

Step Three: Escort Your Child to Bed

When it's time for bed, stop what you're doing and firmly announce, "It's time to get ready for bed," and escort your children through the steps of their bedtime ritual. This eases their worry that you're sending them off alone so you can do wonderful things without them (you are, instead, still involved with them). It also shows them that you mean business. Yelling over the top of your newspaper, "Go on, brush your teeth and go to bed," will never work as well as putting down the paper and walking your child into the bathroom and then into the bedroom. This approach also affirms the idea that the bedroom is a comforting place where Mom and/or Dad give undivided attention, kisses, and hugs.

At first your children may not like this idea of an established and enforced bedtime, and so they may protest loudly. Ignore the complaints and calmly (without ever yelling, threatening, or spanking) walk them through the bedtime routine, even if this means picking them up for an aerial escort.

Step Four: Leave the Room

After you've completed your bedtime ritual, don't linger in your child's bedroom. Say a firm "Good night," and leave the room. Any hesitation on your part will be picked up by your children as a possible indication that maybe you really aren't serious about this bedtime business. No matter how many reasons your children can think of to make you stay longer, finish your routine and then leave. If your children cry and beg you not to leave, assure them that you'll set the kitchen timer for five minutes and will return when it sounds off, but you're going to leave the room now—even if they yell. (If delaying tactics become intense and persistent, see suggested solutions in Chapter Three.)

As you prepare to leave the bedroom, assure your children that they do not have to go to sleep right away. (Remember, it's not your job to put them to sleep.) But insist that they rest quietly in bed. Once they accept this new routine, they most often will be asleep within fifteen to twenty minutes.

Expect your children to protest this plan for at least several nights. But if you persist in remaining calm yet firm, you should see a marked reduction in the length and intensity of bedtime battles within one week. For most families the bad habits war will be completely broken a short time later.

If your child still loudly resists bedtime after one month of consistently using this program, it is likely that the problem is not caused simply by bad habits, but by misunderstood sleep needs or outright rebellion. Chapter Two will give you the information you'll need to deal with these kinds of bedtime problems. If, on the other hand, you find that your child goes to bed, but then continually calls you back or pops up several times during the night, you'll find helpful solutions to these problems in Chapter Three and Chapter Four.

CHAPTER 2

Bedtime Rebellion

Nine-year-old Chrissy Henry was determined to fight for her right to stay up late "like her friends." Her mother, Samantha, was equally determined to end the bedtime war. So, with staunch fortitude, for one month Samantha followed the five-step program outlined in Chapter One. She set a bedtime hour of nine o'clock, establishing a ritual that let Chrissy unwind and prepare for sleep, and remaining firm and consistent. Still Chrissy fought with nightly cries:"I'm not tired." "Why are you making such a big deal about this?" "I won't go to bed!" And on and on. Despite Samantha's efforts, nothing had changed.

If your child, like Chrissy, still vehemently rebels against bedtime after one month of consistently following the program explained in Chapter One, it is obvious that the problem is not simply a bad habit that can be changed by altering the routine. I find that the root of this kind of persistent problem is most often in an inappropriate sleep schedule or in the discipline structure of the family. Nighttime rebellion is likely to develop into bad sleep habits because if, at the end of a long day, you implement the strategies suggested in Chapter One and your child is still obviously ready to argue till dawn, it's easiest to end the tensions by giving in and letting the child stay up late. Hence, habits grow out of forfeit.

Although forfeit is an easier and seemingly more effective solution for stopping evening tensions, there are ramifications of ongo-

17

ing tantrums that lead to late bedtime hours. As explained in the introduction to Part One, these include:

- upset biological rhythms that can cause children to feel disoriented and "off" each day
- physical signs of sleep deprivation such as fatigue, headaches, tension, nonspecific aches and pains, and overactivity
- emotional signs of sleep deprivation such as irritability, lack of motivation, weepy personality, and low frustration level
- negative effect on school performance because sleep loss impairs short-term memory, concentration, and decision-making abilities
- negative influence on parent/child and parent/parent relationships as well as the atmosphere in the home

For all of these reasons and because *you* feel your child needs an established and appropriate bedtime, the following sections will help you determine why your child rebels against bedtime and what you can do about it. (While you're exploring these causes and solutions, be sure to continue to use the bedtime rituals explained in Chapter One. They remain a necessary aspect of controlling bedtime resistance.)

Reasons for Rebellion

If you live with a nighttime rebel, you certainly know that your child doesn't want to go to bed at night. The reasons "why," however, may not be as clear to you. All kids who resist bedtime yell, "But I'm not tired!" so it's difficult to know for sure if your children are getting enough sleep or not. This section will help you determine your child's sleep needs so you can get to the bottom of your bedtime problem.

Circadian Rhythm Problems
Your children's willingness (or more to the point—unwillingness) to go to bed each night may be controlled by their circadian rhythms. We all possess a natural internal clock, called circadian rhythm, which in each twenty-four-hour day synchronizes cyclical changes such as body temperature, hormone levels, and hunger-eating and sleep-waking cycles. When these biological rhythms

work in harmony, we experience a sense of well-being; when they fall out of sync, we suffer consequences that interfere with competent and pleasurable functioning.

Our daily sleep cycle is regulated by these natural ones. We grow weary and crave sleep at the point in the cycle where the body temperature falls. We awake renewed and energized at the point where the body temperature rises to near its peak. The release of the hormone, cortisol, also follows a similar cycle. The secretion of cortisol by the adrenal gland is reduced in the evening and progressively rises to higher levels just prior to our spontaneous waking the following morning. Because of these cyclical changes, when we fall asleep and when we wake are not completely a matter of personal choice.

In Chapter One, I mentioned the average hours of sleep that children at various ages need to stay on track with their biological rhythms. If these averages don't seem to match your children's sleep patterns, you can also evaluate sleep needs, and perhaps pinpoint the root of rebellion, by carefully observing their natural rhythms. How do your children wake in the morning and behave at bedtime each night? If they appear wide awake, argue that they are not tired, fall asleep at an hour later than you would like, and yet awaken spontaneously with energy and in good spirits in the morning, they are most likely rebelling at bedtime because they really are not sleepy. Their circadian rhythms have not yet reached the low point which induces weariness. When this is the case, the established bedtime needs to be pushed to a later hour. How much later depends on how spontaneously the child continues to wake each morning.

Madeline Baxter, for example, has been fighting the bedtime battle with her eight-year-old son since school began last September. "Last summer, we let Alex's bedtime slide up to nine P.M.," she explains. "When I tried to push it back to the usual eight P.M. school schedule, he really gave me a hard time. Because I think elementary school children should be in bed at eight o'clock, he does go to bed at that time, but he still gives me a fight every night. Because he's so stubborn, he rarely falls asleep before nine. I'm just hoping that as long as he's in bed by eight, he's getting the rest he needs.''

Madeline can solve her bedtime troubles by setting a bedtime hour that suits her son's apparent sleep needs rather than one that meets some arbitrary deadline. If a child is in bed at eight o'clock but consistently does not fall asleep until nine, and still wakes in the morning without trouble, nine o'clock is probably an appropriate bedtime.

If you have a similar problem with your children, without altering the ritual, change their bedtime one-half to one hour later. Let your child go to sleep at this new time ten consecutive days. Observe his or her waking mood and state of alertness throughout the day. If on the tenth day your child still wakes without prodding and shows no signs of sleep deprivation (irritability, fatigue, difficulty in concentrating, headaches, or a low frustration level), you can concede to the later bedtime without worry.

Explain to your child that because he or she is getting older, the bedtime can be moved. But then emphasize that this new bedtime is firm. If the arguing continues, then you'll need to set and enforce limits as explained later in this chapter.

Power-Struggle Problems
You can also use your children's natural sleep patterns to decide if they rebel at bedtime simply because they'd rather not go to sleep and so challenge your authority to set limits. Do your children appear sluggish, irritable, or tired at night while protesting that they aren't sleepy? Do they wake reluctantly to the sound of an alarm or only with your forceful prodding? If so, I would say they are fighting their body rhythms at night and being forced to rise each morning while the body temperature and cortisol levels are still at a low point. Whether they will admit it or not, their internal clock is signaling that they need more sleep.

Once you're sure your children need earlier bedtimes, you can confidently assume that their nightly rebellion is caused by a power struggle of authority. In this case, it's time to implement the limit-setting strategies explained later in this chapter.

Naptime Problems
Toddlers who refuse to go to bed at night may also be the victims of

their circadian rhythms. Most children ages two to three need approximately 10 to 13 hours of sleep each day, but because of individual differences some toddlers need to rearrange their sleep and naptimes to keep their cycles in harmony.

By age two, a single late-morning nap is usually the best way to keep the body rhythms synchronized. However, sometimes these toddlers resist the morning nap or the family's schedule won't allow for the sleep break at that time; in these cases, the children often nap later in the afternoon (or fall asleep on the floor watching TV just before dinner). If your 2-year-old takes a late afternoon nap, it is very likely to interfere with his or her ability to fall asleep "on time" at night. If your child throws a bedtime tantrum every time he or she has had a late nap, the problem can be best solved by shifting the nap to an earlier time of the day. If he or she resists the early nap, remain persistent and encourage vigorous morning exercise which can help discharge stored up energies and make an early rest time a welcomed break.

Toward the end of the second year and into the third, many children begin to outgrow their need for a nap. They sleep for increasingly shorter periods and some try to give it up completely. During this period of adjustment, it is difficult to follow a child's circadian rhythms because some do occasionally remain wide awake throughout the day, but then become irritable and crabby by four-thirty or five P.M. the next day. If your toddler seems to have outgrown naptime but then falls asleep from exhaustion too early in the evening, or takes a late afternoon nap and then can't fall asleep at bedtime, you can try to create a more satisfying schedule by setting up a daily, late-morning quiet time. Every day, preferably just after lunch, set simple and clear directions for this quiet time. You might say, for example, "It's quiet time now. You do not have to sleep; you can look at books, or listen to music, or color. But you must stay in your bed, and you cannot get up for one-half hour. If you do this, we'll have a snack together when naptime is over." (A kitchen timer set to ring at the end of naptime helps toddlers understand that the time they must remain in bed is set and cannot be changed by asking, "Can I get up now?") Toddlers who still need a nap will probably doze off before the half hour is up. If they do not, they at least will have an opportunity to rest and this is often enough to carry them through to the end of the day.

You may find that young children will stay in bed or on the couch more willingly if they can see you or if you stop in to reassure them of your nearby presence. At this age, fear of separation can make it difficult to be away from you without this reassurance.

If your toddler is in a day-care environment during the day and he or she is having trouble falling asleep at night, find out how rest time is scheduled. Encourage the caretakers to make sure that rest time is enforced for your child and that late afternoon naps are avoided.

Overtired Problems

Although through careful observation most parents can readily identify their children's circadian rhythms, an overtired child can throw even the most observant parent off the track. This happens because, oddly enough, overtiredness can cause some children to become overly active when a biochemical response to sleep loss increases the release of adrenaline and noradrenaline, stimulating chemicals that fight fatigue. This can be observed quite often in toddlers who miss their naps and in older children who consistently go to bed at an inappropriately late hour.

One mother fooled by this occurrence was amazed that her seven-year-old daughter was so "wide awake" at ten o'clock at night. "Diana would insist that she didn't want to go to bed because she wasn't tired. Although I felt she should be in bed earlier, I gave in to her protests because even at that late hour she would be running and jumping all around the room."

It's only after a reasonable bedtime hour is enforced and the body's natural rhythms fall back into place that parents like this mother see just how sleep deprivation can negatively affect their children. With proper rest, these children become calmer during the day, less likely to fly into whirlwind tirades, and more likely to show normalized signs of weariness at day's end. So if you feel your child should be getting more sleep, but put off insisting on an earlier bedtime because you assume that the high level of late-night activity indicates a reserve of energy, now you know your gut feeling is probably right.

Use the information in Chapter One to give yourself an idea of how many hours sleep your child needs; then roll back the bedtime hour to match. It will take at least a week for your child's internal clock to adjust to the change. So for a while, you may still see signs of hyperactivity. But soon (within two weeks), as your child becomes more accepting of the idea and the body rhythms fall back into harmony, you'll see positive changes.

A BIT-BY-BIT SOLUTION

If the difference between your children's old bedtime and their new one is more than a half hour, they may not be able to reset their circadian rhythms "cold turkey." If they go to bed at this new hour but can't fall asleep until the hour they've become accustomed to, you can help adjust their internal clock by using the bit-by-bit approach.

If your child is old enough to tell time (or can judge time by TV schedules), explain in advance that the bedtime will be moved up ten minutes every night until it lands on the new bedtime hour. To use this strategy effectively, you'll need to move up all bedtime activities. Give yourself plenty of time each night to keep the ritual the same; don't skip any steps and don't hurry the bedtime routine. Do everything the same every night, just change the starting time. A kitchen timer is especially helpful when using this approach because it is a consistent, not-to-be-swayed bedtime signal.

Many families find this bit-by-bit approach quite helpful in making major bedtime changes. However, be aware that if your children are avid TV watchers, this technique may cause more problems than it solves when the timer buzzes in the middle of a "favorite" show. In this case, you may find it easier to move the bedtime hour in thirty-minute increments.

If your children refuse to accept any change in their bedtime and continue to rebel, you'll find help in the discipline technique explained in the next section.

HOW TO SET AND ENFORCE BEDTIME LIMITS

I'm sure you have already set limits, or rules as they're often called, in your home; that's why your children are rebelling. You state the limit "You must go to bed at eight o'clock." Your child says "No" and the fight begins. The trick to setting limits that work is to spell them out in advance, set them according to a three-step program, and enforce them consistently and immediately.

Set Limits in Advance

Don't try to set bedtime limits late at night when you find yourself at the end of your rope. Limits that state, for example, "All right. That's it. I've had it. Go to bed," will not teach your children how to obey those that you set. This kind of limit teaches them to comply only when you're really angry.

In a calm moment *before* bedtime, explain your new plan using the limit-setting instructions discussed below. If you feel your children are old enough, you can encourage them to help you set reasonable limits. As mentioned earlier, your children will be more anxious to abide by rules they help make.

Set Limits in Three Steps

Limits in most American households are one sentence long and begin with the word "Don't": "Don't jump on the couch." "Don't drop crumbs on the rug." "Don't hit your sister." Those that work, however, are stated in three steps and begin with the words, "You can." Because this kind of limit may be new to your disciplinary repertoire, you may make some mistakes and may need some practice, but soon you'll feel confident setting new bedtime limits that:

1. are positive, specific, and impersonal
2. give a reason
3. state a consequence

Step One: Make Limits Positive, Specific, and Impersonal

"Time for bed" sounds like an explicit directive that leaves little room for misinterpretation, but actually it opens the door for rebellion. Your children will be better able to follow bedtime limits if they are spelled out in ways that are positively stated, specific, and impersonal.

• *State Limits in a Positive Way*: You can make bedtime feel less like a punishment by rephrasing the way you announce, "Time for bed." Try not to begin your announcement with a negative thought like, "Remember, you can *not* stay up after eight-thirty." Instead, say, "Remember, you *can* stay up until eight-thirty but then it's time for bed." Likewise, avoid making bedtime sound like you're taking something away from your child with statements like, "You can't watch the next TV show because it's time for bed." Try instead, "You can watch one more TV show; then it's time for bed."

• *Be Specific*: The phrase "time for bed" can mean more than you may initially intend it to. It gives your children the option to decide if you mean, "Time to get into bed." Or maybe, "Time to start getting ready for bed." Or perhaps, "It's time for bed, but you don't have to go if you don't want to." Or even, "It's time to argue your case for staying up later."

When you state your bedtime rules, set specific limits that leave no room for doubt. Include the smallest of details in your instructions. You might say, for example, "You can watch one more TV show, but when the clock says it's eight, start getting ready for bed by putting on your pajamas, brushing your teeth, and picking out a bedtime story. Have all of this done by eight-fifteen and I'll read you the story. Then it's lights out at eight-thirty sharp." This kind of limit helps children be obedient by telling them exactly what you expect.

• *Make Limits Impersonal*: Your bedtime limits should be stated in an impersonal way so that the conflict your children feel when they don't like them is not between them and you, but rather between them and the rule. Stating, "The clock says it's eight," for example, removes the burden of the bedtime announcement from you personally and places it on the clock. Whenever you remind your children about the bedtime limits, don't begin with, "I told you . . . ." but rather say, "The clock (or the rule) says . . . ."

A device like a kitchen timer or an alarm clock works well as an

impersonal limit-setter. Set the timer to signal the start of the bedtime routine and set it again to signal the time for a final "Good
night." Children are less likely to argue against this kind of impersonal limit than against one which comes directly from you and so
promotes the "you against me" feeling.

Such small changes in the way you arrange your words may seem
picayune, but to people who are being told to do something they
don't want to do, it can mean the difference between feeling or-
dered around and feeling in control.

Step Two: Give A Reason

When you take the time to explain the "why" of your new bedtime limits, you appear to your children to be less bossy and more
logical. Because even the youngest children will sometimes rebel
against what seems like an arbitrary order, it's always best to explain your motives.

When you state your reason for the chosen bedtime hour, keep it
simple and keep in mind your child's age and ability to understand. Two-year-olds should understand a simple explanation such
as, "You must go to sleep now so you will feel happy tomorrow."
(They may not agree with it, but they'll understand it.) However,
because most older children would trade in a day's worth of health
and happiness for an extra hour of nighttime play, you need to give
more practical reasons for their bedtime. Help them observe for
themselves how difficult it is to get up in the morning without a
good night's sleep and use the avoidance of that awful "dragged-
out-of-bed" morning feeling as a good reason to get to bed on time.

You can bolster the effect of offering a reason for your bedtime
hour by gaining the support of adults your children respect. Ask a
teacher, grandparent, or your pediatrician to comment to your children on the importance of an appropriate bedtime hour. This can
also serve to put the responsibility for an earlier bedtime hour on
an impersonal "higher" authority. You will face less resistance if
you can say, "I'm following doctor's orders."

You can also use this reason statement to explain why siblings
may have different bedtime hours. You should not send an older
child to bed at an early hour simply because it's easier than trying

to explain to the younger child why he or she has to go to bed before the brother or sister. Establish separate bedtime limit statements and bedtime rituals for each child. Then be firm about enforcing them. Your children will learn that, in many aspects of life, rules are different at different ages. You might make the change to separate bedtimes a bit easier by asking the older child to begin his or her quiet time at the younger child's bedtime. If the children sleep in separate rooms, the older child can read or listen to music behind closed doors without upsetting the younger one. If they share a room then you might give the older child a headboard-light that allows reading without disturbing the sibling. Or, you might let the older child unwind in your bedroom. This remedy keeps the younger child from feeling that he or she is missing out on wonderfully fun activities.

If you calmly and carefully explain why your children should obey a new bedtime rule, but they continue to ask, "Why?" "Why?" "Why?" they are no longer looking for a reason—but rather for your attention. Tell them you have explained the rule and there's no need to explain it anymore. Then continue with its enforcement in Step Three.

Step Three: Give a Consequence

Once your children hear your positive, specific, impersonal, and reasonable bedtime limit statement, it would be nice if they decide to go to bed on time and without complaint. However, if they're in the habit of rebelling against sleep, they probably will not. Children, like most adults, need to be informed of consequences that will motivate them to follow a directive. There are two kinds of consequences you can offer to encourage compliance:

1. Rewards. These are positive consequences that motivate your children to do what's right.
2. Penalties. These are negative consequences that encourage children to do what's right as a means of avoiding something they don't like.

Rewards

It's a basic law of human nature that people tend to repeat acts that bring them pleasure or recognition. At our own jobs, for example, we all have responsibilities that we would like to put off or ignore completely. If completion of these tasks brings us a bonus, promotion, or extra vacation days, we're more likely to get to work with a positive attitude. But if we work for employers who offer no incentives but do threaten extended hours, pay cuts, and reprimands for incomplete work, we become quite hostile and may be prone to cut corners and make excuses. So it naturally follows that if going to bed peacefully at the appointed time brings your children praise and rewards, they are more likely to do it without complaint.

As logical as this seems, we tend to rely instead on punishment as a motivator. Consider, for example, how you would handle a child who was told he must brush his teeth every night before going to bed. If the boy brushes his teeth five nights in a row, but forgets on the sixth, which night would you be most likely to give him your attention? On the night he forgets, of course, because most of us are accustomed to a disciplinary approach that stresses the negative. Before using punishments to end bedtime rebellion (as explained below) give rewards a try. Most children—like most adults—have a better attitude toward doing things if there is something positive in it for them.

Some parents don't like to give rewards because they believe kids shouldn't be bribed to do what's right. But I believe rewards are not bribes. A reward is a compensation for good, meritorious, or desired behavior; a bribe is a payoff to stop inappropriate behavior. For a reward to be effective, first the appropriate behavior occurs, and then the reward is given. ("Get in your pajamas on time and then I'll read you an extra story.") Bribery reverses this order—the payoff comes before the appropriate behavior. So a bribe is given to prevent disobedience from occurring ("Here's a quarter, now stop complaining.") while rewards are things that your children work for, earn, and achieve. That's why rewards give children a sense of accomplishment, not one-upmanship.

There are two types of rewards: social and concrete.

• *Social Rewards*: These are positive consequences that motivate children to behave through the use of praise, recognition, approval, and attention. You may be surprised to find how readily this kind of positive reinforcement can get your children through their bedtime rituals and into bed on time.

Henry Williams, for example, was surprised not only by how well praise worked in coaxing his six-year-old son into bed, but also by how his son seemed so delighted that his dad would notice and comment on things he was supposed to do anyway. "On the first night that I decided to give social rewards," Henry admits, "I thought Jeff would feel that I wasn't sincere and was trying to pull one over on him. But I tried it anyway. I told Jeff to start getting ready for bed by getting into his PJs. After his usual 'Do I have to?' he left the room to get changed. When he came back into the living room, I put down my newspaper and made a fuss over his obedience. I gave him a hug and kiss and told him how nice it is to have a son who is big enough to get himself dressed and do it without having to be reminded several times. At first Jeff looked at me with that smirky smile he uses when he's not sure something is really funny, and then he jumped around the room laughing like I had just crowned him king. I gave him praise and attention after he finished each step of his bedtime routine—by the time it was actually bedtime, he didn't complain at all. I think because I told him he was making me so happy by being good, he was afraid to disappoint me. The next night, Jeff got ready for bed faster than he ever has. After each step, he ran back to me for attention. Before this week, I had no idea how much my approval meant to my son."

Hank is right. Most of us don't realize how motivating a pat-on-the-back can be. The following guidelines, adapted from our book, *Teach Your Child to Behave*, will help you use social rewards in ways guaranteed to reap the best results.

Be Specific

When you give your children social rewards, avoid using vague words like "terrific," "good," or "wonderful." When people make such general evaluations they tend to exaggerate, and so the praise sounds false. (Children are very much aware when they really didn't do what they should do.)

Zero in on and specifically describe the worthwhile behavior that you want to reinforce. Instead of saying, "That was great!" you might try, "I'm really impressed by the way you turned off the TV without complaining."

Also, be sure to praise observable actions of your child, not the whole child. You don't want to damage your children's sense of self-worth by giving the implied message that they are "good" children only when they do what you tell them to. Rather than praise the child's total personality ("You're a terrific kid"), praise his specific behaviors ("I can see you're growing up when you say 'Good night' without whining").

Give Immediately
It is best to give praise immediately. Offer a social reward while your child is in the act, or just finished. As your child walks out of the bathroom, for example, say, "Boy, it's nice when you get washed without complaining." Compliments offered the following morning lose their ability to change behavior. So, although you may not yet be in the habit of giving positive attention to routine tasks, try to remember to use social rewards immediately following the desired behavior so they have a chance to work their magic.

Offer Your Appreciation
Appreciation says, "I like what you did." It indicates that what a child does is valued. Examples of appreciative statements include:

"I'm glad you realize the importance of a good night's sleep."
"I appreciate the way you're trying to follow the bedtime rules."
"I like the way you jump right into bed for your story."

You can also give nonverbal messages of appreciation with a smile, head nod, wink, a gentle squeeze of the hand, a pat on the back, and turning "thumbs up."

Don't Mix Praise and Criticism
You can avoid spoiling the effectiveness of social rewards by staying away from comments like the following which imply criticism:

"It's about time you got ready for bed without having to be reminded ten times."
"It's nice that you got into bed without a fight for a change."
"Well, finally you've done it right."

Social rewards have been proven to be highly effective in their ability to change children's negative behaviors into positive ones. It's these kinds of rewards that you should first use in your attempts to end bedtime rebellion—they can be offered at anytime; they are not costly or cumbersome; they never need to be phased out, and your children will work very hard to get you to use them.

Give Concrete Rewards

Concrete rewards are tangible things or privileges, such as food, money, toys, or special activities that can be used to encourage bedtime obedience. When social rewards aren't enough to change your children's behavior, tagging them on to concrete rewards may do the trick. These rewards are given out based on what's sometimes called "Grandma's Rule," which says, "When you do this, then you get that." You use this kind of reward system when you say, "Eat your dinner, then you can have dessert," and "Clean your room, then your friend can come over." Now, to discourage bedtime rebellion, you can add a consequence to your limit statement that says something like, "If you are in bed by eight o'clock, I'll give you a package of stickers." Or, "If you go to bed without complaining every night this week, you can have a friend sleep over on Friday night."

Obviously, the best kind of reward is something your child likes, but this reward system shouldn't cost you a fortune. Small items that show you're aware of your child's likes and interests should do the trick. Consider, for example, crayons, paintbrushes, or chalk for budding artists. Fishing hooks or lures for young fisherman. Barrettes, headbands, or combs for young ladies. You might also find you can motivate your children with a surprise grab bag. Fill a bag with small inexpensive items that your children like and let them close their eyes and draw one out each night after they've completed their bedtime routine and have said "Good night" without complaint.

It's true that children ages six and older may not be swayed to accept new bedtime rules by small, dime-store items, but they will change their behavior for special privileges. Because it is difficult to dole out special privileges every night, you might try this token reward approach:

Before you begin your new bedtime routine, offer your children a special privilege. Explain that an afternoon at the movies or a pizza party with friends, for example, can be earned by complying with the bedtime rules for a specified period of time. You might begin by requiring three nights of compliance to collect the reward, and then stretch the time period by an additional night every time a privilege has been earned.

You may need to help your children make the connection between their behavior and these kinds of long-range rewards. You can do this by giving them an immediate token reward such as a star or funny sticker every night they go to bed on time and without complaint. These stickers can be put on a chart that will help them keep track of their progress. Seven-year-old, Jan, for example, wanted her school friend to visit the following Saturday. She and her mother worked out a reward plan by which Jan could earn this visit by being in bed by 8:45 every school night that week. Jan's progress chart looked like this:

BEHAVIOR	MON.	TUES.	WED.	THURS.	FRI.
Be in bed by 8:45	★	★	★	★	★

Jan earned her friend's visit and her mom didn't have to argue with her about going to bed. Next week, Jan's parents will offer a smaller reward and so on until Jan is in the habit of going to bed at the appropriate time and no longer needs concrete incentives.

Evaluate Your Reward System

Keep track of how well concrete rewards entice your children to get ready for bed on time and without protest. If the rewards you're using aren't working, don't give up this positive approach. Find a more powerful reward or vary the rewards you offer so your children don't lose interest. Remember, the first steps toward bedtime obedience are the hardest ones to take and so they deserve special notice.

To make rewards effective you must also be sure that in the early stages of this approach, they are offered every night. An on-again-off-again reward system will not convince your children to change their behavior for any length of time. Only after bedtime rebellion is a thing of the past and peaceful bedtimes become habit should you begin to give the rewards less and less frequently until you finally phase them out completely.

Make It Fun

Rewards not only are good motivators, they can add fun to otherwise boring nightly routines. Younger children, especially, enjoy marking off their bedtime progress on a picture chart. To make this kind of chart, draw pictures or take photographs of your children as they complete each step of their bedtime rituals: brushing teeth, putting on PJs, setting out the morning clothes, reading a story, etc. Paste these pictures along the left side of a piece of posterboard. Then, as your children complete each task, let them put a star next to the appropriate picture. You might want to combine this practice with token rewards by promising that these stars can be exchanged later for a special prize. But very often the fun of earning stars and the pride of accomplishment may be motivation enough to encourage your child to get ready for bed with a smile each night.

You will find your older children rushing to get ready for bed when they play Beat-the-Clock. Start this game a half hour before your children's final bedtime by setting the timer for fifteen minutes. Tell your children, "If you get yourself ready for bed before the timer rings, you can stay up and play for the rest of the half hour. If you don't beat the timer, then you'll have to go to bed right away and there'll be no more playtime until morning." If your children beat the clock (and they surely will once they realize you really will put them to bed early if they don't), reset the timer for their bedtime and let them play quietly until it rings again.

Studies repeatedly find that immediate positive reinforcement is the best way to control bedtime resistance. A recent study out of Arkansas Children's Hospital found that social rewards offered after each step of the preparatory routine helped eliminate the power struggles between parent and child which typically occur at bedtime. These researchers also found that when compared to the use of penalties, positive routines produced the fastest improvement in decreasing the tantrums of children. Also, because the positive approach reduces family stress, this study found that a significant number of involved parents who used social rewards, rather than penalties, noted an improvement in both their marital relationship and the number of daily, positive interactions with their children.[1]

For these reasons I recommend that you first use the reward system to stop bedtime rebellion. If you find that the positive approach is not working with your child, then you might try enforcing your bedtime limits with the Drawing-the-Line approach described in the next section.

PENALTIES

Penalties are negative consequences. They are the unpleasant things that happen to your children if they break the bedtime limit you set. Penalties are the most common disciplinary tactic used in most households and yet they remain the most controversial. At some time, all parents wonder, "What's an appropriate penalty?" "How much is enough?" "How much is too little?" "Will penalties make my child hate me?" The answers to these questions are difficult to pinpoint because they depend on many factors such as which rule is broken, the number of times the child has disobeyed the rule, the parents' emotional makeup, and the quality of the parent/child relationship.

It is known that most penalties are not effective in controlling bedtime rebellion. Scoldings just make everybody angry and they don't seem to have any carryover effect to the following nights. Taking away privileges (such as TV or playtime) doesn't make a dent in the problem because, since it's bedtime, the loss can't be enforced until the following day; by that time the ability of a consequence to change behavior may be gone. And physical punishment (spanking, hitting, slapping, etc.) is not an effective way to teach children how to behave.

Innumerable studies concur that physical punishment is not an effective disciplinary tactic. It does not accomplish any of the goals of discipline which include the intention to: (1) change negative behaviors to acceptable ones in the long run, (2) encourage children to develop modes of self-discipline, (3) teach children the logical and natural results of misbehaving, or (4) nurture a close parent/child relationship. Most parents use physical punishment when they can't think of a better way to correct a problem. Parents always tell me that it's when they're at the end of their rope and feel they're losing control that they resort to spanking, hitting, and the like. I have written this book to offer you better ways.

Drawing-the-Line

Drawing-the-Line is an approach to bedtime enforcement that combines the strategies of ignoring and room restriction. I have repeatedly found these strategies to produce long-lasting effects in stopping bedtime rebellion.

• *Ignoring*: Ignoring is a disciplinary approach that seeks to change rebellious behavior by completely disregarding children's tantrums until they eventually fall asleep. Because some children can scream longer than parents can ignore, a more bearable strategy, called intermittent ignoring, also has been found to be effective and yet less upsetting to use. To use this technique, you must ignore the tantrum for a short period of time (perhaps five minutes); then go and check on the child, and then resume ignoring for another five minutes, after which you'll repeat the cycle. Each night you increase the amount of time between check-ins. Responding to the tantrum after the specified period of time can make ignoring children's crying easier for you because these check-ins assure you that they are physically okay and it also assures them that they have not been abandoned.

If you choose to use the ignoring method, explain to your children how the plan works. Long before bedtime, sit them down, get their full attention, and firmly and calmly inform them that starting that evening you expect them to go to bed at the scheduled time. However, if they choose to carry on and cry about that, it's their choice and they can yell all they want, but you plan to ignore the noise.

That evening, continue to follow your nightly rituals and offer positive reinforcement. Then at the bedtime hour, say "Good night," and leave the room, ignoring the crying. If your children are still crying after ten minutes, you can go into the room for a fifteen second check. Do not offer any undue attention: do not hug, kiss, or comfort. Simply put your children back into bed if they are on the floor, tuck them in, and leave.

• *Room-restriction*: If your children run out of the room after you, you'll need to implement the room-restriction phase: escort or carry your children back to bed without saying a word. Remind them that they are restricted to their room at bedtime and then leave. Repeat this procedure every time they come out of the room. If your children will not stay in the room no matter how often you return them to bed, warn them that the next time you have to bring them back, you will close and lock the door. (Some parents feel more comfortable enforcing room-restriction when they install a screen door in the child's room so he or she can see out.) Explain that you will not open the door until they get into bed—they may still be crying, but they must be in bed before you can open the door. This gives them a choice in the situation. Once you give the warning, follow through if they come out of the room again. Remind them that they are in control of the door. If they continue to try to get out, the door stays closed. If they get into bed, the door will be opened. If the bedroom door does not lock from the outside, attach a chain-lock or a hook-and-eye lock on the outside to secure it.

Repeat the check-in procedure every ten minutes until your children finally stop crying and drop off to sleep. The next evening, follow the same routine, but extend the time between check-ins to fifteen minutes, the next night to twenty, and so on until your children learn to go to bed and stay there without protest.

If you decide to use this Drawing-the-Line approach, be sure to follow two general rules of penalty enforcement. First, stay calm. Your limit statement is all you need to set down the rule and carry out its enforcement. Each night, remind your children of the limit, the reason, and the consequences of following or disobeying the bedtime rules, and then carry through. There's no need to yell, scream, or hit. Stay in control and quite matter-of-factly enforce the promised consequence. The goal of bedtime discipline is to teach your children how to go to bed and stay there. In doing so, you do not want to make your children feel "bad" or unloved. A calm but firm approach is much more likely to convince them that you believe an appropriate and peaceful bedtime hour is important because you care about their health and well-being, not because you're a hostile and enraged person who has to have your own way.

Second, don't carry a grudge. You can continue to promote a caring and concerned attitude by making an effort to start the following morning on a positive note. Children have a tendency to feel rejected and unloved when penalized by their parents. So use a hug and a smile to show your children that you still love them and want to relate to them in positive ways for the rest of the day.

Drawing-the-Line does work. It is noisier and more stressful than positive reinforcement, but for some exceptionally stubborn children, it brings more rapidly effective results.

GENERAL ENFORCEMENT RULES

Whether you offer positive or negative consequences to enforce your bedtime limits, there are two rules that will always apply: enforcement of consequences must be done consistently and they must be done immediately.

Be Consistent

When you offer a reward or penalty, make sure you are willing and able to carry through one hundred percent of the time. You should not, for example, say you will lock the bedroom door if your children come out again, but then give them "one more" warning when they appear in the living room. Also, you can not ignore their tantrums one night, and resume arguing and pleading the next. These inconsistencies sabotage your efforts. In the same way, you should plan to offer rewards every night for the same activities. If you reward every step of the routine one night, and ignore the completion of those same steps the next, you'll weaken your ability to change behavior with positive attention.

Give the Consequence Immediately

Promise consequences only when you're sure you can give immediate delivery. Don't, for example, offer a reward that you don't have in the house. A package of stickers given as soon as the final "Good night" is completed will serve as an effective concrete reward. The promise of getting such a reward some time the following day after you get to the store to buy it, is a strategy that will lose its motivating impact if and when it lands in the child's hands. Also, don't say you're going to lock the door or ignore tantrums "as soon as your father gets home." Any delay, such as "When I finish this report," "When I get off this phone," or "When your grandma leaves," will diminish the power of the negative consequence.

SUMMARY

Bedtime rebellion can be stopped if you make and enforce a limit in three steps. Although it has taken an entire chapter to explain all the ins and outs of effective limits, the actual implementation of this approach is quite simple. To review:

1. State the bedtime rule in a positive, specific and impersonal manner.
2. Give a reason.
3. State a consequence.

For example, a limit statement intended to stop the bedtime tantrums of a 6-year-old boy might read like this:

Limit: You can play until eight o'clock, but when the buzzer rings, then it's time to brush your teeth, get into your pajamas, go to the bathroom and get into bed by eight-thirty.
Reason: You have school in the morning and you need to be awake and alert to learn.
Consequences: If you're in bed at eight-thirty, you can take something out of the grab-bag. If you're not in bed, I will escort you into the bedroom, you can not have a toy from the bag, and I'll ignore your yelling for the rest of the night.

If bedtime rebellion has made your evenings resemble scenes from the battlefield, rest assured that you are not alone in your nighttime problem. Bedtime resistance is consistently the most common complaint expressed to pediatricians each year. It is a problem that grows out of bad habits, ineffective discipline systems, and ongoing power struggles between parents and children. Whatever its cause in your home, this three-step limit-setting approach will help you end bedtime bedlam.

CHAPTER 3

Delaying Sleep

You've done it! It's eight o'clock and the kids are in bed; the house is quiet and you sit down to relax with a novel you've been dying to read. But then at 8:10 it starts. From the bedroom, comes the cry, "Mom, come here. I have to tell you something."

8:20: "Dad, I need a glass of water."

8:45: "Mom, did you wash my blue pants? There was a quarter in the pocket."

9:05: "I have to go to the bathroom."

And on and on until you've completely lost track of the novel's plot, your patience is gone, and you scream for all the neighbors to hear, "GO TO SLEEP!"

Delaying tactics like the ones above are passive forms of bedtime rebellion that don't rely on noisy tantrums or arguments. Instead, they're like the rhythmic sound of a slow-dripping faucet that seems only mildly annoying at first, but eventually becomes an intolerable nuisance.

As you surely know, the methods children use to delay the moment of sleep commonly begin with the words, "I need another . . . . " You can then fill in the blanks with an array of needs ranging from the traditional "glass of water" and the heart wrenching "kiss and hug," to the quest-for-knowledge "story" and the dare-you-to-ignore "trip to the bathroom." Whatever the excuse, the bottom line on delaying tactics is that they are another form of bedtime resistance.

39

If your children routinely try to delay sleep, you can be sure that they won't suddenly grow out of the habit. Delaying sleep is an art practiced by children since the beginning of time and so now, at this turn of the century, they're really quite good at it and enjoy perfecting its use still further. However, like other bad bedtime habits and bedtime rebellion, delaying is a practice that shouldn't be tolerated because it robs children of the sleep they need for healthy physical and psychological functioning and it interferes with the time that should be reserved for you and your spouse. To end nightly delaying tactics, you'll first need to take some time to consider their cause.

REASONS FOR DELAYING

By far, I have found the most common reason for delaying sleep to be the fact that children don't want to call it a day. The remedy for this kind of general resistance is the focus of this chapter. But before you assume this is the reason, take time to consider some of the causes explained below that could indicate that your child's persistent stalling has other roots whose remedies are explained elsewhere in this book.

Separation Anxiety
Separation anxiety is an intense, emotionally fearful reaction experienced, at one time or another, by most children when separated from their parents. The transition from being awake to being asleep is difficult for children prone to this fear because sleep does take us "away" from those we love. If your child is between the ages of eighteen months and three years, separation anxiety should be considered as the first possible cause for delaying sleep. It should also be considered if your child has recently been ill, or if he or she has experienced a traumatic event such as a divorce or death in the family.

If you feel that intense separation anxiety could be the cause of your child's efforts to delay sleep, the disciplinary approach outlined in this chapter is not an appropriate first-step solution. Instead, read Chapter Seven; it will help you decide if your children call out because of a true psychological need or simply because they resist the idea of going to sleep.

Trouble Shifting Gears

Some children continually call out from their beds because they're too wound up to sleep; bringing their parents back into the room keeps the action going. This bedtime problem can usually be resolved by changing the routine to include quiet time which helps children unwind before it's time for sleep.

Before using the limit-setting technique explained later in this chapter, first try to solve the problem by building a quiet time into your children's bedtime routine. To allow time for unwinding: (1) avoid roughhousing for at least one hour before bedtime, and (2) explain to you children that after they get washed and into their PJs, they can read or color or listen to music in their beds for (at least) fifteen minutes but then it will be time for sleep. This gradual change from being active to lying still in bed may be all your children need to shift gears smoothly without repeatedly calling out.

If, however, your children go to bed in a calm, quiet, and peaceful mood, and yet still call out to you, then perhaps they really aren't tired. As the next section explains, the root of delaying can sometimes be found in an inappropriate bedtime hour.

Wrong Bedtime

Children who aren't ready for sleep because their internal clock hasn't yet begun to slow down will be very tempted to call out from their bedrooms simply because they're bored. If your children appear tired, irritable, or sluggish at bedtime, you can be reasonable sure they need to go to sleep at that bedtime hour. But if they appear wide-awake and really can't fall asleep, they may be working against their body's biological needs. The discussion of circadian rhythms in Chapter Two will help you decide if your children are genuinely not tired or just trying to delay sleep.

Wanting Attention

We all know that life in the modern American family is often hectic. And so it's not unusual for bedtime to arrive long before our children have had a chance to fill their daily attention quota.

When this happens, they will relentlessly call out after their bed-time for "one more" anything that will bring them a few more coveted moments with Mom or Dad. If, for example, the evening was rushed and the kids were briskly hustled off to bed, and now Mom is on the phone, kids will call out questions, problems, and requests just to force her attention away from the phone onto them. Or, if Dad usually comes home a half hour after the chil-dren's bedtime hour, they may keep yelling out just to ensure that they won't fall asleep before Daddy gets home.

Although time is undeniably tight, if you find that your chil-dren call out most often on nights when you have been especially busy and haven't given them much undivided attention, try to keep this in mind as you map out your daily schedule. Put off some of your housework or paperwork until after the kids' bed-time so you have more time and energy for them. Then, stay involved in the bedtime routine and use it to give extra hugs and pats-on-the-back. It often happens that when children's needs are met during the day, they're more willing to go to bed without a struggle. If you give them this attention at bedtime and they still resist sleep, at least you'll know that they aren't calling out for you to fill an emotional need.

If you can not find anymore "quality time" than you're already squeezing out of your day, just be aware that this fact could be the reason your children call out and crave some time with you at night. Tell your children you understand the way they feel, and when you set bedtime limits (as explained later in this chapter) perhaps you can offer incentives that promise more time together on the weekends.

Bad Habits

Most children who tenaciously call their parents back to their bedrooms for "one more" of something are practicing a learned behavior. They have learned that, even though you sound annoyed or even angry, if they keep stalling you'll probably re-ward the call not only with the requested drink of whatever, but also with your attention, another good-night kiss, and another tucking-in routine. That makes the effort worthwhile. Like gam-blers who occasionally win a dollar or two in the quarter slot machine, your children persist in the hope that maybe, one of these times, they'll again win the prize—your attention.

Unintentional parental reinforcement of this habit is the reason most children successfully delay sleep. Fortunately, in the same way these children learn they can gain parental attention by inventing excuses to bring them back into their rooms, they can learn that calling out will no longer be rewarded. The rest of this chapter will focus on the limit-setting method that helped one particular family end the disruptive calls from the dark.

SETTING NEW LIMITS

You can squash the bad habit of delaying sleep by following the same limit-setting procedures described in Chapter Two. To review how limits are set in three steps and enforced calmly and consistently, let's take a look at the case of a seven-year-old boy whose father, John, is a friend of mine. The boy, Matthew, has always resisted bedtime, but because his parents insist, he is in bed at 8:30 sharp every night. However, at 8:31 he begins his delaying routine which usually goes something like this:

"Dad! Is tomorrow Saturday?"

"No, go to sleep."

"Mom! My sock has a hole in it."

"I'll give you a new pair tomorrow. Go to sleep."

"Dad! Come here; I have to tell you something."

"Matthew, it's time for bed. Now stop calling me and go to sleep."

"But it's important."

"This is the last time I'm coming in. If you have anything else to ask me, ask now."

"Mom, I need a tissue."

"All right. Get one from my dresser."

"Dad, I think my bed is broken. Come here."

"It's not broken, go to sleep."

"Yes it is; look!"

"This is the last time I'm coming into your room. Do you understand?"

Twice in this typical scenario, Matthew was able to get his dad into his room; that's reward enough for a seven-year-old trying to put off sleep.

After an especially aggravating night, John told me about the problem and agreed to set the following three-step limit to try to stop his son's delaying routine.

Step One: Make Limits Positive, Impersonal and Specific

You'll recall from Chapter Two that when setting a limit it should be stated in a way that makes it positive, impersonal, and specific. So several hours before the bedtime hour, John sat down with his son to explain the new rule. He made it:

- *Positive*: "Before you go to sleep you can go to the bathroom, bring a glass of water to your room, keep your own box of tissues on your night table, and ask me any questions on your mind. But . . . "
- *Impersonal*: ". . . when the timer buzzes at eight-thirty, that marks the end of . . . "
- *Specific*: " . . . calling out, asking for things, asking questions, getting out of bed, or in any other way delaying sleep."

Step Two: Give a Reason

Then John gave Matthew a reason for this new bedtime rule: "I'm enforcing this rule because when you call out to us so many times each night, you don't get to sleep until a time much after your bedtime which is supposed to be eight-thirty. You need a full night's sleep to do your best in school."

Step Three: State a Consequence

To complete the third step of limit setting, I encouraged John to use praise and an incentive technique called tapering. To do this he told his son:

> "If you do not call out after I've said 'Good night' at eight-thirty, I will come back into our room to see how you're doing every fifteen minutes. But if you do call out, your mother and I will not answer your questions and the fifteen minutes wait starts all over again."

This tapering approach is an often-used technique that makes behavior changes appear less drastic than a "cold turkey" plan. The new rule is easier for Matthew to accept because it doesn't completely take away the attention he's used to getting; it does, however, require him to change his behavior to get it.

LIMITS IN ACTION

Each morning John called me to report his progress. Although he had doubts about the approach in the beginning, tapering, along with daily praise, broke Matt's habit of delaying sleep in just four nights.

• *Night #1.* On the first night that John set the new bedtime rule, Matthew called out at eight-thirty-five, "Is fifteen minutes up yet?" Without entering Matt's room, his dad calmly but firmly answered, "No, but now the fifteen minute wait starts all over again. I'll set the kitchen timer for fifteen minutes again. If you don't call out before it rings, I'll come in to check on you."

For the next hour, Matt didn't call out to his parents, and John faithfully checked in every fifteen minutes. At nine-thirty Matt was asleep, but at this point, John wasn't impressed with the plan. Although his visits were brief (less than thirty seconds) and without affection (no hugs or kisses), Matt had made himself stay awake so he wouldn't miss his dad's appearances. John thought the plan gave his son more reason to stay awake and it left him with even less time to relax with his wife. But still, because he had agreed to try this approach for one full week, the next morning he praised Matt's efforts and encouraged him to do as well that night.

• *Night #2.* On the second night, John reminded Matthew of the rule and told him that he would again visit every fifteen minutes. This apparently seemed too long a wait for Matt; for an hour and a half (until he finally fell asleep), Matt stubbornly called out to his parents even more frequently than before the new limit was set. John, however, calmly and consistently kept his end of the deal by resetting the timer every time Matt yelled out and also by refusing to answer any questions or to give attention by arguing.

The next morning, John told Matt it was too bad that he

couldn't visit him last night, but then he assured his son that the next time it would work out better.

• *Night #3.* On the third night, John reminded Matt of the rule and fifteen minute periods between visits. When the kitchen timer sounded the arrival of the first visit, John promptly went to his son's room. Matt was sitting up and smiling. John jostled his son's hair, praised his obedience, and promised to visit in another fifteen minutes if he didn't call out before then. When John went to Matt's room for his second visit, he found his son sound asleep. Matt was learning that there was no reward in calling out anymore and that he could get his parents' positive attention only by lying still.

• *Night #4.* On the fourth night, John again praised Matt's obedience of the night before and set the timer for fifteen minutes. When John went to Matt's room after the first fifteen minutes, he found his son sound asleep.

After the fourth night, there was no need for John to set his kitchen timer. Tapering, along with daily praise, helped Matt break his delaying habit in just four nights. There will probably be nights in the future when he'll try to delay sleep again, but his parents now know how to enforce limits that will keep these attempts from becoming a habit.

OTHER INCENTIVE IDEAS

Some children will need more time than Matthew to give up their delaying tactics, but if praise and tapering are an appropriate consequence for your children and if you use them consistently, you'll see positive results in one week. If you don't, you might need to offer more concrete rewards like those described in Chapter Two, or you might try offering one of the following two incentives that have worked well with other parents I've counseled:

• *Payback Time.* Payback time is an incentive method that requires your children to pay back the time they delay sleep. (It is most effectively used with children who can tell time.) If, for example, bedtime is set for 8:30 and they call out to you at 8:35, they then owe you five minutes of sleep time. To pay back this time, the following night they must be in bed at 8:25. If they call out again that night at 8:45, they owe you twenty minutes of sleep time the following night.

This method will usually not motivate children to stop calling out until the moment of payback arrives. If you consistently enforce the earlier bedtime, they quickly learn you mean business and really do expect them to lie quietly in bed after the first "Good night."

• *Tokens to Keep*. This incentive method gives children complete control over their own rewards. Before you say "Good night," give your child four small token rewards; these may be nickels, toy rings, stickers, barrettes, crayons, etc. Explain that every time your child calls you back into the bedroom, you will take one of the rewards away with you. If, for example, your child calls out, "Mom, can I have a glass of juice?" go to the bedroom, remind your child of the rule, and take one reward away. If your child calls out again, "If I'm quiet, can I have my sticker back?" go to the bedroom, again restate the rule, and take another sticker away.

This method causes some crying and pleading the first night or two, but if you calmly and firmly carry out your end of the bargain, it will not be long before your child is content to lie still and keep all the rewards.

Like all concrete reward methods, the tokens must be phased out eventually. Over time you reduce the number of rewards offered until there is no more need for incentives. Once your child is well accustomed to falling asleep without delaying, you'll find the habit broken and social rewards can be easily substituted for the tokens.

TIPS TO MAKE IT WORK

Before you crack down on your child's incessant delaying routine, take time to think about the three steps of setting an effective limit. Write them down to make sure you're stating them as clearly and as simply as possible. Then consider how motivating your consequences will be. Finally, use the following three tips to help you plan ahead how you'll enforce the consequences you set.

• *When Necessary: Use Room-Restriction Strategies.* When you first begin to ignore the calls from the dark, your children may assume you can't hear them. That's when they'll test your resolve by coming out of their bedrooms to ask their questions and make their nightly requests. When they first do this, immediately escort them back to bed without fuss or argument; remind them of the bedtime limit and say "Good night," and leave. If they continue to venture out, then you'll need to use the room-restriction method explained in Chapter Two on page 35.

• *Stay Calm.* When children are in the habit of baiting you to get your attention, even negative attention will fill their needs. That's why if you threaten or yell and holler at a stubborn child, you unknowingly sabotage your efforts to withhold your attention. No matter how your child responds to the new bedtime limits, stay calm. Enforce your rules in a matter-of-fact manner that will make it clear you are not engaging in a power struggle— you're simply doing what's best.

• *Be Consistent.* It's important to enforce the promised consequences *every* night. If you say you'll be back in fifteen minutes, don't forget to return. If you say your child owes you ten minutes in payback time, be sure to collect the next night. If you offer a concrete reward for the following day, make sure it's there to give.

As you set out to break bedtime delaying habits, you'll quickly find that calm and consistent enforcement of the limits you set is the key to success.

CHAPTER 4

Nightwaking

All parents look forward to the time when their infants will sleep through the night. Friends are often quick to ask new parents, "Does she sleep through the night yet?" Office workers good-naturedly kid sleepy-eyed colleagues, "Guess the baby isn't sleeping through yet, huh?" And a most common question asked of pediatricians at even the first check-up is, "When will he sleep through the night?" What is not so commonly discussed, however, is the older child who never does learn to sleep through the night or who does but then suddenly reverts to nocturnal wakings. Untold numbers of children over one year of age regularly wake during the night and either call out for their parents to come into their room and help them go back to sleep, or leave their own beds and sleep with their parents.

THE REASONS THEY WAKE

As mentioned earlier, waking during the night is not unusual. As we all alternate between light and REM sleep (named for the rapid eye movements that occur while dreaming), we tend to wake for brief periods every night. When children wake and fall back to sleep, as we do, we don't notice or feel there is a problem. But when children wake and then wake us to help them go back to sleep, then it becomes a family problem that disturbs everyone's sleep.

49

I believe the key to solving this problem is in understanding why some children need their parents when they wake and others do not. Like bedtime resistance, rebellion, and delaying, nightwaking happens because young children quickly fall into bad bedtime habits that are difficult for them to break without your help. The nightwaking habit often begins in very early childhood or even in infancy when parents first teach their children to associate certain conditions, like rocking or feeding, with falling to sleep. The habit can also develop later when bedtime practices, such as falling asleep in the living room, become the rule rather than the exception. Once a sleep association is made, children need these conditions present whenever they fall asleep and again in order to fall back asleep in the middle fo the night.

For example:

- Five-year-old Lauren will not go to sleep at bedtime unless one of her parents sits at the foot of her bed. Lauren calls them into her room almost every night because when she wakes, the prop she associates with sleep is no longer there.
- Three-year-old Timmy goes to sleep each night to the sound of lullaby music his mom plays on the tape recorder near his bed. She turns off the music after he's asleep, so when Timmy wakes later in the night, he can't go back to sleep without calling to his mother who then plays the music again or sits by his side until he falls asleep.
- Seven-year-old Melissa falls asleep on the couch in front of the TV every night, and then her dad carries her into her own bed. When she wakes during the night, the TV isn't on and her parents aren't around; so to help herself fall back to sleep, Melissa goes to where her parents are—in their bed.
- Four-year-old Robert slept in his parents' bed for two weeks when they went on vacation to a small one-bedroom bungalow. Now back at home, he wakes every night around midnight, runs into his parents' room and slips into their bed. If his parents tell him to sleep in his own bed, he cries until they give in and let him sleep in theirs.

As you can see from these examples, nightwaking is a learned behavior often taught by parents themselves. But, fortunately, just as you may have been helping your children maintain poor sleep associations, you can teach them new ones that will let them fall back asleep without bothering you when they wake during the night.

CHARACTERISTICS OF NIGHTWAKERS

Although children wake their parents during the night for many reasons, studies have found a pattern that identifies children most likely to be nightwakers. Researchers have found that nightwakers are usually children who:

- have no regular parent-organized bedtime routine
- are difficult to manage at bedtime
- control when and how they go to bed
- have parents who remain with them until they fall asleep
- fall asleep in living areas and then are transferred to bed
- have parents who repeatedly respond to their calling out or crying
- have parents who stay with them until they're asleep or take them into their own beds when they wake at night.[1]

Do you and your child fit any of these? If you do, it is most likely that your child's nightwaking is a bad habit that *can* be broken with the strategies suggested later in this chapter.

If your child does not fit into any of the above categories, but still wakes and calls for you on a regular basis, he or she may be experiencing a physical or psychological problem which probably cannot be resolved with the discipline approach presented here. See Part Two of this book for a discussion of these kinds of sleep-disrupting problems.

DON'T WAIT FOR THEM TO OUTGROW IT

Children do outgrow the nightwaking problem. (Healthy teenagers do not habitually wake their parents!) But, as encouraging as "they'll outgrow it" may sound, I feel that for several reasons it's not advisable to wait for your children to outgrow this problem. Years of interrupted sleep is a literal nightmare for all members of the family and so, while you're waiting, nightwaking can take its toll on everyone's physical and psychological health.

As explained in the introduction to this section, sleep is vital to our physical well-being. Nightwaking children and their parents suffer the obvious signs of sleep deprivation which include fatigue, headaches, irritability, lack of motivation, whining, clinging, and impaired ability to concentrate. In addition, once nightwaking becomes a habit, many parents and children adjust to the interrupted sleep schedule and assume that their sense of habitually feeling "off" is normal for them. It isn't until their children begin to sleep through the night that parents realize just how dramatically sleep-loss can affect daily functioning. Many notice a positive change in their attitudes and daytime interactions with their children after the children learn to sleep through the night. Parents also see improvement in their children's daytime behavior; commonly reported changes include observations that the children become "happier," "easier to handle," "less aggressive," and "more settled."[2] The thought of getting a good night's sleep is probably quite appealing from your point of view; knowing that it will do the same for your children should help you stand firm in your desire to do something about this nighttime problem.

Sleep training (as teaching a child to sleep through the night is sometimes called) is also considered important to children's psychological development. Parents who leave their own beds to soothe their children when they wake in response to natural sleep cycles, complicate their children's ability to separate from their parents without anxiety. Many parents enjoy sleeping with their children in what has come to be called "the family bed." In some circumstances, however, parents who allow their children to share their beds add anxiety to the separation process. This is especially so when one parent who can't sleep with the thrashing child leaves the bed to sleep elsewhere, or when a separated or divorced parent allows (or even encourages) a child to sleep in the absent spouse's place. This usurpation confuses children's view of their role in the family and hampers the development of a clear and separate identity. To become independent and autonomous, children must eventually learn that they have a place in the family that is separate from their parents, also that they are safe even when they're apart from you at night. When you teach your children how to put themselves back to sleep at night, you also teach them all these things.

Without a doubt, children benefit from sleep training in physical, social, and psychological ways. As an added benefit, sleep training can improve your marriage since in very obvious ways nightwaking causes marital tensions. Often parents don't agree that there is a problem, or they blame each other, or don't agree on the problem's cause or solution. One parent may insist on completely ignoring the night-crier and the other may worry that such ignoring will cause psychological damage. The parent who can't sleep because of the crying or the up-and-down movements of the comforting parent, or the kicking child in the marital bed, may abandon that bed for a quieter sleeping place. It is not surprising that in these circumstances which create tired, resentful, and angry people, marital harmony doesn't flourish.

In more subtle ways, nightwaking keeps unhappy spouses from constructively dealing with their problems. A spouse can avoid intimacy by claiming, for example, "I had to sleep in Billy's room last night because he wouldn't stay asleep unless I was there." Allowing children to sleep between parents is another way of subtly driving a wedge between couples. If you are resisting the idea of teaching your child to sleep through the night in his or her own bed, take careful inventory of your marital situation. If your marriage is a shaky one, you may be subconsciously aware that sleeping children may force you to face your problems, thus your reluctance.

THE SOLUTION

The solution which I find most effectively ends the nightwaking problem combines a number of behavior modification approaches into one program. This program will help you give your children appropriate sleep associations and set three-step limits that tell your children what you expect from them during the night and what they can expect from you. The goal of this program is to teach your children the skill of falling back to sleep without your help. Like all other skills you have taught your children (like walking, talking, and toileting), the perfection of this ability will take some time and patience. But with consistent use, you should see a reduction in nightwaking problems within one week.

Set New Bedtime Routines

A few rare nightwakers go to bed at a scheduled time, without complaint, and without their parents' help. Most, however, have fallen into bad habits that may appear only mildly annoying at bedtime, but become unbearable when they need to be repeated in the middle of the night. To end the nightwaking, you'll need to look first at exactly how your children fall asleep each night. Do they sleep in front of the TV? Do you stay in their bedroom until they fall asleep? Does your younger child take a bottle or pacifier to bed? If your children fall asleep under any circumstances that they themselves can not easily duplicate when they wake at night, your efforts to teach them to sleep through the night must focus first on an initial bedtime routine that will teach them to fall asleep without your help.

A full discussion of the importance, creation, and implementation of bedtime routines is presented in Chapter One. You might want to review the details, but in summary: a bedtime routine should start at least a half hour before the bedtime hour. It should involve a sequence of events that are followed in the same order every night. It should include a quiet time for talking or for a bedtime story. When the routine ends, you should say "Good night" and leave the bedroom while your children are still awake.

If this procedure is quite different from the way your children now go to bed, your plan to adapt a routine and to change the way you respond to nightwaking should begin with a family discussion before the bedtime hour. At this meeting explain to your children the new nighttime plan and then set your limits as mapped out in the next section.

Set Three-Step Limits

The new bedtime limits aimed at stopping nightwaking should follow the same three steps used to reduce other forms of bedtime resistance. To begin:

• *Set A Limit*: Like those intended to stop other bedtime problems, limits to stop nightwaking should be positive, impersonal, and specific. A *positive* limit explains what your children *can* do.

Try to offer options that encourage your children to use objects or routines that will help them make the transition from being dependent on you to being self-soothers. You might say for example, "You can sleep with all your favorite stuffed animals." Or, "You can sleep with a night-light on." Or, "You can keep a flashlight next to your bed." Or, "You can come into my bed when the sun comes up." These "can do" statements help your children accept new limits because they are offered something in return. If, in the past, your children have associated sleep with props like the TV or your presence in their bedroom, you'll now need to use an *impersonal*, third-party limit setter to get them into their own bed and asleep without these aids. Add to your positive statement something like, "But when the kitchen timer (or my watch, or the clock-radio, etc.) says it's nine o'clock, you have to get into your bed." Experience tells me that your children won't like this rule so you should be prepared to stand firm despite their objections. Chapter Two focuses solely on the rebellion that can follow your insistence on a scheduled bedtime hour without your presence in the room. If your nighttime trouble starts at bedtime, be sure to read and follow the suggestions in that chapter because children cannot be taught to fall back to sleep in the middle of the night until they learn to be self-soothers at their initial bedtime.

Once children learn to put themselves to sleep with self-soothing methods, they may begin sleeping through the night without any further training on your part. But if, even after they've learned to fall asleep in their beds without your help, they still call out for your or come into your bed during the night, the following limit-setting formula will quickly teach them to kick the habit.

When you set the details of the new nighttime limit, be *specific* about exactly what you mean by "sleep through the night." It would be a mistake to tell your children that they can't wake in the middle of the night anymore. We all wake and even after successful sleep training, your children will continue to do so. Tell them, instead, that if they wake, they cannot wake you. Tell them specifically, "Don't call out to me. Don't ask me to come into your room, and don't come into my bed. You have to stay quietly in your own bed until you fall back to sleep."

• *Give a Reason*: Once the habit of nightwaking is established, it's hard for children to understand why it can't continue. You can try to explain the importance of a good night's sleep, or the unhappiness caused by fatigue, or the privacy entitled to married couples, but the best reason for setting limits on nightwaking is really quite basic. Explain to your children that although during the day you answer their calls, comfort them when they're sad or worried, and fill their requests, you won't do these things during the night because nighttime is for sleeping. Simple as that.

• *State Consequences*: As obvious as this reasoning may seem to you, your children will certainly protest the idea. Don't let this sway your decision to teach them this skill. Just as you haven't let your children's protests stop you from enforcing other limits that are necessary for their health and well-being (like the ones against sticking hairpins in electrical outlets and eating ice cream for breakfast), you should not be unnerved by children who challenge the wisdom of this plan. You can, however, ease the shock of the new bedtime rules and fortify your position by explaining to your children that there are both positive and negative consequences for obeying or disobeying them.

• *Positive Incentives*: Social rewards are a very effective way to shape new middle-of-the-night habits. Even if, for example, you have to take your child out of your bed and put her back into her own ten times in the course of one night, you can encourage better results the next by praising her for sleeping in her own bed all night (even though it wasn't exactly her own idea). You can also promise to call Grandma or some other special person in the morning if your child follows the nighttime rules. Children will also be proud of even the slightest nighttime improvement (and therefore anxious to repeat the act) if you praise their "grown-up" efforts in front of older siblings. And, of course, when your children do start sleeping through the night, you can encourage the continued progress by commenting on how wonderful and happy *you* feel now that you're getting a good night's sleep.

You can also use concrete incentives to encourage your children to sleep through the night. You might offer morning rewards such as a favorite breakfast, a trip to a fun place, or a visit with a special friend. To help your children over the especially difficult first few nights, you might even award a toy prize first thing the following morning. (But remember, don't promise rewards you can't immediately deliver.)

A progress chart that keeps track of successes and that promises a very special reward after a given number of days may sway older children to lie silently through the night. For example, you might initiate the limit on Monday night and promise a pizza (or sledding, fishing, picnic, or swimming) party as a reward on Saturday. Draw a star chart like the one on page 32 and tell your children that every star they earn represents another friend they can invite to this party. If, on Saturday morning, they have successfully slept through two nights (a likely number within this time period), then call up two friends and celebrate! If you do choose to keep a progress chart, remember: award stars only for completely successful nights. Social praise is an appropriate reward for "trying," but giving stars for trying weakens the motivation to strive for success.

• *Consequences*: Although positive incentives may encourage your children to comply with the new nighttime rules, it's also necessary to discourage noncompliance. The consequences for nightwaking are tailored to the particular nighttime problem, so if your child disrupts your sleep by calling out during the night appropriate consequences are explained below. If your sleep is disrupted by a nightwaker who wants to climb into your bed each night, the consequences for this behavior begin on page 60.

• *How to handle a child who calls out during the night*: The strategy I recommend to stop children from calling out in the middle of the night is determined and consistent *ignoring*. When you explain this new nighttime approach to your children, expand your statement of the limit, the reason, and the reward with this warning: "If you do call out, not only will you lose your reward, but I will completely ignore your calls and crying." Stress again the fact that nighttime is for sleeping and that you will not get up in the night.

Ignoring is a strategy you may have already used to stop other negative daytime behaviors like whining or temper tantrums. Sleep training by ignoring is an extension of this kind of discipline. If you feel ignoring a daytime temper tantrum is an appropriate form of discipline despite the initial and often escalated screaming you may have to endure, then you can see why the method can eventually stop the nighttime tantrums that may occur when you no longer respond to the calling out.

The first night you institute the new nighttime limit you'll probably find that your children don't believe a word you've said. Because it's still their habit and they haven't yet learned that they can fall asleep without your help, they will continue calling out to you. When you ignore their calls, they'll probably start crying and eventually move on to screaming. Most children will try anything to get you into their room as they have been able to do every night in the past. Head banging, breath holding, vomiting, toy throwing, etc., may all be attempted to make you offer your attention.

If you hold your ground and ignore the commotion, eventually, most children will come to get you. At that point you can continue the ignoring tactic by appearing to be so sound asleep you can't hear a thing. Or, if the noise becomes too great or your children begin to physically hurt you or themselves, you can calmly, firmly, and without offering any attention, escort them back to their room, restate the limit, and go back to your own bed. If your children again come to get you, then you'll need to use the room-restriction strategy explained on page 35 to keep them confined to the bedroom.

In theory, ignoring is a simple and effective method of sleep training. The method is straightforward in its one-step, can't-make-a-mistake structure, and studies continually attest to its high success rate. However, in practice, I've known it to shake the resolve of even the most determined parent. To bolster your chances of success I suggest that before you use this tactic, plan how you'll handle the stress of hearing your children cry out, "Mommy, I need you. Daddy, help me."

A clear understanding of why you want your children to sleep through the night will reinforce your decision when you're tempted to call it quits. Doing what's best for your children is often the difficult route, but still you wash bloodied knees despite screaming protests and you bring your children to the baby-sitter or preschool even though they scream, "Don't leave me!" In the dark of the night, when you know it would be easier just to give in to the cries, remind yourself that teaching a child to sleep through the night independently is also something that is done for his or her own good.

Knowing this gives you good reason to ignore complaints in the night, but actually doing it can take some creative forethought. Cynthia Reynolds, for example, was determined and prepared. After successfully teaching her three-year-old daughter to sleep through in two nights, she wrote me a letter detailing the experience. With her permission, I'd like to share some of it with you.

Dear Dr. Schaefer,
Well, the first night was awful. Christine cried so pathetically and kept calling my name. The reason she couldn't sleep to begin with is because I've always run in to comfort her at the slightest sound so it made me feel so cruel to just ignore her. At first I just lay in bed listening. But I knew I'd never make it through the night doing that so I turned on the vacuum, put on ear phones and listened to soothing music. I didn't have to worry about anybody else because my husband was away on a business trip and Christine's brother was spending the night at his grandma's. I also didn't worry about Christine hurting herself because earlier in the day I baby-proofed her room and took out all the breakable stuff like you suggested and although I couldn't hear her, I never took my eyes off the door of her room.

After about ten minutes she came running into my room and threw a tantrum. She ran around, threw herself on the floor, and rolled about kicking her legs like crazy for another ten minutes. I pretended I was sleeping through the whole scene. Then she tried to climb into my bed so I carried her back to her room and started to close her door. That really made her scream! So I told her if she got into her bed and stopped crying I'd leave the door open, but if she didn't, the door would stay closed. I closed the door and held the knob so she couldn't open it. She started kicking the door and yelling at me. When she calmed down for a second, I said I'd open the door only when she got into bed. Then I heard her get up on her bed; I opened the door and right away she jumped down again. I quick shut the door and again she started crying. I told her to get back in bed and I'd open the door. She did, so I opened the door, reminded her about the new bedtime rule and I went back to bed (and turned off the vacuum and tape player). I don't know if she slept from exhaustion or because she gave up trying to get me to come sit by her side, but after a bit of soft weeping, Christine slept the rest of the night.

The next night, I was again prepared with my vacuum and music. When Christine first started crying for me to come sit by her, I lay still waiting to see how upset she'd get. I couldn't believe what happened: after about five minutes of yelling, there was silence. I was worried she might have hurt herself (you wouldn't believe the horrible things I thought she might do to herself) so I tiptoed to her door to peek; I knew if she saw me I would have ruined the whole thing, but I couldn't sleep until I knew she was okay. There she was sound asleep hugging the new doll I bought her to sleep with (I had tried to convince her that her new baby needed her to sleep quietly).

This morning I gave her the reward I promised and she seemed so proud to have slept without me sitting on her bed. It broke my heart to let her cry like that, but the smile on her face this morning helped me see it didn't hurt her and was all for the best.

Thanks,
Cynthia

Cynthia's concern about feeling "cruel" is a common reaction to letting children cry; you may even worry that sleep training may cause your children psychological damage, but there is absolutely no evidence to support that idea. If you explain your plan in advance and you give plenty of love and attention during the day, there will be psychological growth rather than damage done from teaching a child one of life's most basic facts: Nighttime is for sleeping. Cynthia may still hear some night-crying from her daughter, but they've gotten over the toughest part and I have no doubt that the whole family is now feeling much happier and better rested.

• *How to handle a child who comes into your bed*: When you first try to keep your children in their own beds, you might use a rather subtle tactic called crowding. Explain to your children that there just isn't enough room in your bed for them to sleep comfortably and offer them positive incentives to stay out. If, however, the promised reward isn't enough to keep your children in their own beds and in the dark of the night they steal into yours, don't say anything, but make their visit a very uncomfortable one. Pretend to be asleep, stretch your arms out over their faces, roll over, and push them to the edge of the bed; if they fall out, don't say a word. If your children climb in between you and your spouse roll toward the middle and squish them just enough to make it a very unpleasant place to sleep.

Relentless crowding is sometimes enough to convince children they'd rather sleep in their own bed and earn a reward at the same time. If however, your children don't take the hint after two nights, then it's time to try another negative consequence.

Remind your children of the limit and explain that if they do come into your bed, you'll bring them back to their own. Tell them up front that if they come into your room one hundred times, you'll return them to their beds one hundred times.

In actual practice, you may need to return especially stubborn children ten to twenty times the first night (but it will seem like a hundred). Obviously, this will interfere with your own sleep, so be sure to begin the method on a weekend or holiday when you and your spouse don't have to be at work early the next morning. No need to tire yourself with arguing, however. Every time your children come into your room, return them immediately, state the rule, and leave. Don't beg, plead, yell, discuss, hug, kiss, spank— give no attention or sign of emotion at all.

It's important to catch your children before they get into your bed because, although you must still return those you find sound asleep next to you, the goal is to give them the experience of falling asleep in their own beds by themselves. Every time they doze off beside you, they take one step away from this goal.

If you find that your children are especially adept at sneaking in without waking you, you'll need to set up some kind of alarm system. Some parents I've worked with have partly closed their bedroom doors and put bells on the knobs; others put bells on their children's doors so they can intercept nightwanderers before they get any where near their parents' beds. You can also position a chair or door wedge so it will be hit by the opening door. I don't however, recommend locking your own bedroom door because it is never safe to let a child roam through the house alone at night—especially an angry child.

I also advise against solving the nightwandering problem by locking children in their rooms all night. A locked door can be a very frightening approach if the child has no control over the door. Instead, if your children run back out of the room faster than you can return to your own bed and you're tired or carrying them back to theirs, you might find the perfect solution in the room-restriction strategy explained on page 35. Room-restriction gives children ultimate control over their own door: if they stay in bed, the door stays open; if they get out of bed, the door is closed.

It sometimes helps to let your child rehearse the nighttime consequences you include in your limit statement. During the day, you might, for example, pretend you're asleep in your bed and then instruct your child to try to climb in with you. Stand up immediately, state the rule, and escort your child to his or her room. Do this cooly and without discussion so that although it's a game, your child gets the picture that it's not a fun one. Then let your children pretend to be you sleeping in your bed. Try to climb in next to them and let them get up, repeat the rule, and bring you back to their bedroom. Younger children might like to practice the return-to-bed routine with their dolls or stuffed animals. These rehearsals may make your children giggle, but they also give them a concrete picture and a better way of remembering what they can expect during the night.

While practicing this technique with your children, you can also increase their willingness to stay in their own bedrooms by making those rooms more attractive and interesting places to be. During the day, let your child help you clean the room, rearrange furniture, and redecorate. If they share the room with siblings, give them a special corner that's "theirs;" this helps children see the room as a safe and special place that belongs to them. Try to maintain this image by avoiding any daytime punishment that ends with "Go to your room." These kinds of punishments tend to make children associate their bedrooms with punishment, which works against your goal of making them want to stay there.

REGRESSION

Once you have successfully taught your children to sleep through the night, it would not be unusual for them to suddenly wake and call out or appear at your bedside again. If this happens, take a moment to evaluate why the nightwaking problem has returned. When children who experience a frightening dream, a traumatic life event, illness, or even a difficult developmental stage seek comfort in the night, it should be considered a sign of normal emotional regression and you can certainly give them the comfort they need. However, be careful to keep the exception from turning back into a habit. Many children see once as an exception but twice as the new rule.

If you can find no reason for the renewed nightwaking (and your children can't come up with one either), they're probably experiencing a natural period of skill regression. When learning any new skill, children will often take five steps forward but then one step back. Most children, for example, will have an "accident" weeks after being completely toilet trained; some will stop talking soon after their parents boast about their growing vocabulary, and many school children will grasp a math concept but then feel baffled by the same kind of problem two months later. The skill of sleeping through the night is no different.

You can keep this regression from becoming another ongoing battle by immediately reenacting the nighttime limit you initially set. In fact, you may find the information in this chapter will become a handy resource over the years as your children periodically test your decision to make the night a time for quiet and peaceful sleeping.

SUMMARY

If your children wake you at night by calling out and insisting that you come into their rooms, you can break this habit if you:

1. establish a nighttime routine that teaches them to fall asleep without your help. (See Chapter One for specific details on setting bedtime routines.)
2. set a three-step limit that sounds something like this:

a. "You can sleep with all your stuffed animals, but in the middle of the night you can not wake me or call me to come into your room. If you wake and it's still dark out, you must lie quietly in your own bed and go back to sleep."

b. "I want you to do this because nighttime is for sleeping and we both need our sleep."

c. "If you sleep until the morning without waking me, we'll call Grandma and tell her how grown-up you are now and you can have this new coloring book and crayons. If you do wake me, we won't call Grandma and you can't have the prize. I also won't answer you. I'm going to ignore your calls no matter how loudly or how often you call; I'm going to sleep all night tonight."

If your children wake in the middle of the night and then jump into bed with you, you can break this habit if you:

1. establish a nighttime routine that requires your children to fall asleep in their own beds without your help.

2. set a three-step limit before they go to bed that sounds something like this:

   a. "You can come and sleep in my bed in the morning when the sun comes up, but you can not come into my bed during the night."

   b. "You can't come into my bed anymore because when you do, neither of us get a good night's sleep because the bed gets too crowded."

   c. "If you sleep in your own bed all night, you can have this new cartoon pillowcase. If you do try to come into my bed before the sun comes up, you can't have the pillowcase and I won't let you in the bed. From now on I'm going to keep bringing you back to your own bed until you learn to stay there."

If you consistently enforce these limits you and your child should be soundly sleeping through the night within three to seven days.

PART II

Bedtime Fears

We all are afraid of some things. Fear of danger, fear of hunger, fear of being alone are all normal, healthy feelings that enhance our lives and challenge us to provide for our own safety and security. Your children too experience normal fears that are appropriate at various developmental stages. But because these fears are often different than our own, we may dismiss them as "silly" or worry that they are indicators of deep psychological problems.

The four bedtime fears discussed in this section are all predictable signs of growth in children. You can be reasonably sure that fear of the dark, of night monsters, of separation, or of nightmares will upset your children's sleep at some time before they reach adolescence. When it happens, you'll be witnessing concrete evidence of the sense of vulnerability that accompanies growing independence. Then just as predictably, in most cases your children will outgrow the fear and move on to their next developmental conquest.

However, knowing that bedtime fears are inevitable doesn't mean they should be ignored. When children experience bedtime fears, their sense of terror is real and they need you to teach them how to cope with these feelings. Saying, "There's nothing to be afraid of," is confusing to a frightened child and it doesn't offer any guidelines for dealing with the unpleasant experience.

On the other hand, being overprotective of a fearful child is also an inappropriate solution. If you seek to end nighttime fears by taking your children to your own bed, by lying in their beds, or by allowing them to sleep on the couch by the TV, you'll again miss the opportunity to teach them how to face and manage their own feelings.

Learning to manage fear is an especially important skill. Studies are finding that fears are now found more frequently among young children than they were a decade or so ago.[1] Although this fact may be due in part to parents' increased willingness to report children's fears, there is also evidence that there is simply more to be fearful of. I have seen many children whose bedtime fears are caused directly by overexposure to negative adult problems and behaviors. High achievement expectations, media-relayed horrors, news accounts of violence against children, family dissolutions, and increased family mobility are all reasons to expect fears in our children and to be prepared to teach them how to handle these feelings. You'll find that when your children learn to conquer their bedtime fears they will become generally more confident and capable of coping with many other day-to-day problems.

In the following chapters I've provided you with step-by-step guidelines for helping your children learn how to control bedtime fears. Before you plunge into a suggested program, however, take some time to evaluate the degree of fear being experienced by your children. Some bedtime "fears" are actually stalling tactics or passive forms of bedtime resistance. Many a clever child has managed to worm her way back into the living room and one more TV show by claiming, "I'm afraid." Other times the fear is real but mild and is most easily allayed simply with comforting words and perhaps a nightlight. It is when the fear is intense and physically evident in signs like paleness, shaking, rapid breathing, dilated pupils, and/or real tears, or when it follows a bad experience like being locked in a dark room or chased by a dog that you'll know your child needs to learn the coping skills outlined in each chapter in order to reclaim the peace of sleep.

At the end of each chapter you'll find a list of suggested readings under the heading "Bibliotherapy." Bibliotherapy is an approach to fear management that uses stories to illustrate another person experiencing and solving a given problem. The goal is to give insight into the situation and to bring about in the reader a change of attitude. I have seen bibliotherapy successfully used in many areas of child development. There are books, for example, about toilet training that follow a young child through the fears and apprehension of using the toilet and on to full mastery and the accompanying feelings of pride and accomplishment. There are also books which teach children how to handle their fear of going to the doctor, the dentist, the baby-sitter, school, a new house, or even to get a haircut. In the same way, stories about other children experiencing and conquering bedtime fears will help yours feel less alone or different for having these feelings and can give them the courage they need to face the problem. Although bibliotherapy is usually not an effective method of fear management in itself, when combined with the other tactics suggested in each chapter it can support your child's efforts to sleep tight.

CHAPTER 5

Fear of the Dark

Fear of the dark is probably the most common childhood fear. (Studies have found that it affects up to seventy-five percent of all children by age four and up to ten percent of children between the ages of four and ten.) It's a developmentally normal occurrence which can often be resolved simply by putting a low-watt light in the bedroom until the child outgrows the fear. However, for some children, fear of the dark becomes a serious problem that can't be resolved with a night-light, but, instead, requires more active involvement on your part. This chapter will help you decide if your child's fear goes beyond the norm and, if it does, what you can do about it.

WHO'S AFRAID?

Your children will probably need your help to overcome their fear of the dark if they:

- are over the age of five
- show an intense fear that may be marked by frightened cries at bedtime and/or in the middle of the night
- will not stay in their own room more than one minute if the light is turned off.

For example, six-year-old Brittany has a problem that can't be resolved with a night-light and can't be ignored. Brittany never complained about going to bed until very suddenly one night, she yelled out when her mother turned off the light as usual. Brittany began to cry and she begged her mom to leave the ceiling light on. No amount of assurances could convince her that there was nothing in the dark to be afraid of. Now, three months later, Brittany still wants the light on every night. If her parents turn off the light after she's asleep, she cries hysterically when she wakes later in the night.

It may seem that leaving a light on is the best way to solve nighttime problems like Brittany's, but persistent or intense fear of the dark can have negative side-effects that make it wise to teach these children how to deal with the dark.

REASONS TO TURN OFF THE LIGHTS

I don't believe there is any reason to deny a child a small nightlight in the bedroom. But if he or she wants to combat fear of the dark by leaving bright lights on all night, this solution causes other problems for both the child and you. To begin with, fear of the dark is an irrational one that can terrorize children when circumstances such as blackouts or childish pranks by friends. Even an absentminded flip of the basement light switch unexpectedly throws children into the dark. Younger children experience extreme terror in these kinds of situations, while older children, who find themselves in these circumstances outside the home or when they're with friends, feel extremely embarrassed by the way they react to the dark. Because of this fear of the dark and of embarrassment, many kids cannot go camping with their friends or even enjoy a sleep-over party. In these ways the fear is destructive to a child's sense of self-esteem and growing feelings of independence. And so, when the fear is persistent or intense, it's best to confront it, deal with it, and put it in the past.

Because fearful children lose sleep time, it's also best to reduce their fear for health reasons. Children who sleep in a well-lit room often become light sleepers. This deprives them of the deep sleep stages they need each night. Also, children who are afraid of the dark require almost four times longer to fall asleep than nonfearful children. This means that the average falling-asleep time of twenty minutes can run more than an hour for children with this fear. They often wake and call out to their parents in the middle of the night, causing them to lose even more sleep. This sleep loss eventually adds up to daytime fatigue, irritability, and weepiness which by nightfall can make them feel even more insecure and fearful. The cycle can't be broken until the child overcomes the fear of the dark.

Parents, too, feel the effects of a child's night fears. Many children insist that the parents sit beside them until they fall asleep; this obviously takes away from the parents' personal time. Other children wake in the night and run to their parents' bed to escape their fears. The family bed is a controversial issue in itself, having both advantages and disadvantages (see page 52). But it is known that in some circumstances sleeping in the parents' bed can complicate the separation process and cause marital arguments and tensions if one spouse is displaced or upset by a third body in the bed.

Unfortunately, the methods some families use to help their children cope with their fear can cause even more problems. It's not uncommon for children to trade in their fear of the dark for more stubborn, bad bedtime habits. As explained in Part One, "putting" a child to sleep by sitting on the bed, or by letting him or her fall asleep on the couch or in the parents' bed can very easily foster a bedtime habit that soon has nothing to do with fear. Instead, it becomes the circumstance the child associates with sleep and which must be repeated each night so he or she can sleep. Certainly, fear of the dark is a very real one that needs to be handled with compassion. Unless the fear is dealt with properly you can get stuck in nighttime routines that cause chronic bedtime resistance, rebellion, stalling, and nightwaking.

When Jimmy was four-years-old, for example, he suddenly developed a fear of the dark after watching the movie *Aliens*. His parents tried to assure him that the aliens were make-believe and couldn't harm him, but still Jimmy wanted the light left on. Just past midnight, he arrived sobbing at his father's side of the bed. Eager to comfort his son, Jimmy's dad put him in bed between himself and his wife; Jimmy fell back to sleep feeling safe. The following night, he again went to sleep with the light on and again later woke his parents and asked to sleep in their bed. His parents gladly offered him the security of the light and then their bed. Now, two years later, Jimmy has long forgotten about the alien creatures; he's no longer afraid of the dark, but he still sleeps in his parents' bed three to four nights a week. No amount of coaxing or pleading can keep him out. If, when Jimmy's fear of the dark first became evident, his parents had used solutions like those suggested in this chapter rather than continuously taking him into their bed, he would have learned how to conquer the fear in his own room and his parents would not now be living with the fatigue of sleep loss caused by a fidgety eight-year-old in bed with them.

There are also a few very practical reasons to address the fear of the dark problem. If, for instance, your fearful child shares a room with siblings, even a low-watt light burning all night can disturb them and/or cause them, too, to develop a sleep association between a bright room and sleep. And lastly, there is the cost over time to burn and replace the light bulbs that stay on all night.

Perhaps the most important reason to teach your children how to overcome their fear of the dark is your own awareness that they would be happier, better rested, and more self-assured if no longer victimized by the dark.

HOW TO TURN OFF THE LIGHTS

There are two notable methods of helping children overcome their fear of the dark. I've presented them here in what, in my professional experience, is their order of effectiveness. You can choose one method over the other because it best fits your style of parenting or nighttime routine, or you can combine several tactics that you feel will best comfort and encourage your child. Whichever method you choose, you'll need to remember to reassure your children that you understand their feelings; remind them that you will always be nearby to protect them, and express confidence in their ability to overcome the problem.

Systematic Desensitization

Systematic desensitization is a fancy psychological term for slowly and gradually introducing people to the object or circumstance they fear until they feel comfortable and unthreatened. You may have heard, for example, that people who are afraid of flying can be trained to conquer their fear in small steps that first bring them to an airport, then to the entrance of the plane, then into the plane itself, then to a seat, then to a shuttle out to a runway with an immediate return to the terminal, and then finally to actual flight. With this same method of taking small, gradual steps you can help your children overcome their fear of the dark.

In part one of this process, you will gradually reduce the level of illumination in the child's bedroom. You can do this by periodically changing the main light bulb to a lower-wattage one, or by using a much easier and recommended method in which you change the degree of illumination with a rheostat dimmer switch, available at any hardware store for less then twelve dollars. It replaces the standard on/off wall switch and its dial gradually dims or brightens the degree of light in a room. Once the switch is installed, mark on the dial with a pencil or crayon eight degrees, evenly spaced, between the brightest and darkest settings. This will guide your progress as you gradually lower the illumination.

The night you plan to begin the desensitization process, explain to your children that you've thought of a game that will help them get over being afraid to sleep in the dark. Focusing on the "fun" aspect of this game, tell your children that on the first night they can put the dimmer switch on any setting they'd like. If they choose the brightest setting, that's fine.

The following night cheerfully explain that you are now going to lower the light just one notch. Tell them that when they sleep through the night with this reduced illumination without yelling out, you will reward them in the morning with a prize. (Reveal exactly what the prize will be and make sure you have it available to give them immediately upon waking.) If your children call out or wake you in the middle of the night, offer them comfort, but do not offer them the prize in the morning. Do, however, give positive assurances that they will do better that next night. If they do sleep through the night, give them their prize as well as praise for the accomplishment.

Leave the light setting at that mark until your child successfully sleeps through for three nights without obvious signs of fear. Then move the dimmer dial to the next lower setting and follow the same routine (praise and reward included) for three more nights. As this program of desensitization moves along, children will gradually adapt to an ever-darkening room.

Finally when the brightness level reaches the lowest mark on the dial just before complete darkness, plug a night-light into an electrical outlet in the bedroom and use that in place of the main room light. (Use a night-light with a bulb rather than one with an illuminated figure.) You may want to progress to the darker, illuminated figure night-light, or to a completely darkened room, or a darkened one with a night-light in the hall or bathroom, but a child who sleeps comfortably through with only a night-light can no longer be considered to be afraid of the dark.

During the next few weeks, continue to praise your children the first thing each morning. Comment how proud you are; at the breakfast table, boast in their presence about the deed to other family members. And each night say "Good night" with positive expectations such as, "I know sleeping in a darkened room is no problem for you now. You're so grown-up."

In part two of the desensitization process, you'll help your children change the fearful associations they've made by offsetting them with fun and games played in the dark. The following are a few in-the-dark games you can play with your children just after nightfall during the same time period that you're gradually lowering the room's light. I don't recommend, however, that you play these games immediately before bedtime. Any bedtime routine should be spent quietly unwinding. For children who are afraid of the dark it will be overstimulating to play in a darkened place and this will complicate their efforts to fall asleep easily without fear.

• *Hide-and-Seek*: This hide-and-seek game doesn't involve hiding in the dark and then jumping out to scare the person doing the seeking. Instead, to play this game, hide a toy or a stuffed animal in your child's room. (If you hide a new toy as a prize, inexpensive items like crayons are best because you may want to play this game several nights and it shouldn't cost you a fortune.) Then encourage your child to hold a flashlight and go with you into the darkened room to hunt for the hidden object. The next time you play, switch roles and let your child hide the toy. (Encourage him or her to do it while the lights are still off, but if that causes a problem, turn them on.) Then, by yourself, go into the dark room with a smile and show that you feel comfortable and even happy as you seek the object. On the next night, hide an object again and ask your child to hunt for it without you; if you get resistance, go along on the hunt to help him or her feel braver. Keep playing the game until one night your child willingly ventures into the dark alone.

• *Follow-the-leader*: This game follows the standard rules of the game, but the course at some time will go through the dark bedroom. As the leader, you might, for example, start in your lighted bedroom and hop over the entryway into the hall, then, heading toward your child's room, walk backwards for several feet. Switch to a side step until you reach your child's dark room; without slowing the pace of the game, bravely march into the dark room and then come out to complete the circuit back to your bedroom. (At first, you might just dart in and out of the dark room, and then increase your stay each time you play.) Then, let your child be the leader, making sure that he or she knows the game must go into the darkened bedroom. If your child merely runs in and out, follow along the same way; each time you play, the time in the dark will surely get longer.

• *Count-in-the-dark*: If your child is old enough to count, you can play this game which records quite concretely how slowly but surely your child is adjusting to staying in the dark without fear. To begin, say to your child, "Let's go into your bedroom without turning on the light. We'll hold hands, count to five, and then race to see how fast we can turn the light back on." Each time you play, count to a higher number. When your child becomes more accustomed to the dark, suggest that you play the game clapping your hands to count out the numbers. (Letting go of hands will help ease you out of the game.) Later, suggest that you each take turns sitting in the dark while the other stands at the door and counts out the numbers. When your child can sit alone in the dark to the count of one hundred, her fear of it is conquered.

The successes your child experiences playing these games should parallel your work with dimming the light each night. If, for example, your daughter can sit in the darkened bedroom to the count of one hundred, but the light dimmer switch is still up on one of the highest degrees, you should not wait three nights to move the dial down a notch; move it one notch each night. But be careful: even if your child seems quite happy to play these in-the-dark games, don't lower the wattage more than one notch per night. Rushing the process can cause a setback when your child settles in alone and realizes it's too dark.

The success of systematic desensitization depends on consistency. *Every* night, remind your children of their goal, state positive expectations, praise past progress, lower the room's illumination gradually, and comment on all accomplishments every morning. Inconsistent use of this routine will drastically reduce the likelihood of success. If he or she sleeps every other weekend at Grandma's where the overhead light once again stays on all night, your child probably won't be able to come back home and pick up at the level where he or she left off. If you know there will be nights when your child will sleep away from home in the month following your first night of desensitization, it may be best to use a bedside lamp rather than the dimmer switch. Then as you reduce the illumination of the bulbs from one hundred watts to seventy-five watts, to sixty watts, etc., you can send the bulb (and the lamp if necessary) with your child when he or she sleeps away from home. If you remain consistent in our reduction of light levels and in your offering of praise, your children should be "cured" of their fear of the dark in one month's time.

COPING SKILLS

Another way to combat fear of the dark is through a series of coping skills. Because this approach requires the voluntary involvement of the child and assumes the child wants to overcome the fear, it is most successfully used with those who are at least five years of age. The following three coping skills have been found to work most effectively when used in combination just before the final "Good night." They may be used as a tactic in themselves or may be combined with the desensitization program explained above.

• *Relaxation*: Think how your body would react if you saw your child dash into the street in front of an oncoming car. Your voluntary muscles would immediately tense in fear. Because it is physically impossible to be relaxed and scared at the same time, relaxation exercises help children confront and deal with their fears. Choose one of the following relaxation methods and use it consistently. If you find it's not working, then try another but don't use too many at once as this would be time-consuming and perhaps frustrating to your child.

You can encourage your children to feel relaxed at bedtime by stopping all roughhousing, discussion of discipline or school problems, and scary or exciting TV shows one hour before. Set this time aside for calm and quiet activities such as reading, music, talking, and card or board games that are not overly competitive.

Once in bed, you can help your child physically relax body muscles. Although children generally can't concentrate long enough to follow the plan of progressive muscle relaxation that is used to help adults relax and reduce the pain of childbirth, you can play a few games that will help ease tensions. If your children are familiar with marionettes, you can encourage them to relax and tighten their muscles as if they are a puppet whose strings are released and then pulled tight. Or, some children are very responsive to muscle massage; you can firmly but gently stroke and knead the large muscle groups in their arms and legs to bring on a state of relaxation. You can also ask your children to lie down and inhale deeply and then think the word "relax" as they exhale. Encourage them to do this five times each night just before you turn out the light and leave the room. Tell them to repeat the exercise five more times after you're gone; this will keep them from tensing up because they're alone.

Finally, to enhance the relaxation exercise, tell your children to smile as they lie in bed. It's quite difficult (if not impossible) for your children to experience frightening thoughts or tense their muscles in fear while they're smiling.

• *Positive Self-Statements*: These are the things we tell ourselves that make us feel braver, happier, more efficient, etc. They can effectively counter the terribly frightening things that most people say to themselves when they are in fearful situations.

Imagine, for example, that you're terrified of being alone in the house at night during thunder and lightning storms. When you find yourself in this situation, you begin to imagine the worst things that could possibly occur. You go around checking all the locks and then turning on all the lights so the house appears to be full of people. You periodically check the telephone to assure yourself that the lines haven't been cut. As you do these things, you talk to yourself saying, "Oh no, I hate being alone at night. What if the power goes out? What if someone breaks in? I'm so scared. What will I do?!" You say these things until finally you're so scared you pull a blanket over your head and lie on the couch immobilized by fear, and still the frightening thoughts continue.

Your children go through the same kind of self-dialogue when they lie alone in the dark. But you can teach them how to talk to themselves in ways that will squash the fearful thoughts. Every night, before bedtime, help your child practice saying statements aloud like, "I am brave and I can take care of myself in the dark." "I am safe in my bedroom with my mom and dad close by." "It's okay to be a little afraid; I can handle it." "The dark is my friend and the best place to go to sleep." Practice the statements over and over each day so it will be second nature for your child to start talking positively when he or she becomes fearful at bedtime.

• *Positive Imagery*: Like positive statements and relaxation exercises, positive imagery helps or child replace fearful thoughts and reactions with pleasant ones. As your children lie in bed, tell them to close their eyes and imagine themselves doing something they enjoy. This may be something like bike riding, swimming, or playing with friends. Help your child build up an entire scene that is enjoyable in every way. Your child should think of this same scene every night so you might want to write it down and read it back to your children at bedtime.

Recently, I met with a seven-year-old boy who was described by his mother as being scared of the dark. For six months he had been calling out during the night, sleeping with the light on, and often sleeping in his parents' bed. After our initial consultation, his mother decided she would like to try to help him overcome his fear with coping techniques. She began nightly relaxation exercises, positive statement rehearsals, and positive imagery. Kevin's positive image may give you an idea of the kind of scene I'm talking about. It read like this:

> "I'm in the park playing soccer with my dad. My friend Joey is there too. The sun is shining and there's a breeze that keeps us from getting too hot. I run down by the goal and Joey kicks the ball across the field to me. I give it one good kick and it goes right past Dad and I score! Dad can't believe he missed it and Joey runs up to me and we give each other a high-five shake. We're laughing so hard we fall down on the ground."

Every night when Kevin would tell this story or his mom would read it to him, he found himself smiling at the end. Tell your children to replay their image in their mind any time they begin to feel afraid. Like positive self-statements, this method keeps your children from focusing on fearful thoughts.

Another approach to using positive images involves your children's superheroes. Let your children create a scenario in which their favorite heroes are assigned special guard duty in their rooms. The hero can be imagined to be stationed in the corner of the bedroom all night to protect sleeping children from harm. (If you use this superhero approach, don't let the hero fight off the evils or monsters of the dark. Your overall goal is to convince your children that there are no evils or monsters in the dark to fear.)

With consistent use, these three coping strategies—relaxation, positive self-statements, and positive imagery—can help children overcome their reluctance to stay in the dark at night. Kevin's mother combined the coping strategies with the desensitization games described above and found that after six weeks Kevin was no longer afraid to sleep without a light and he no longer came into her bed in the middle of the night.

REWARDS

Whether you choose to help your children overcome their fear of the dark with systematic desensitization or coping skills, always reward their efforts. Use praise freely; repeatedly tell your children how glad you are that they are making an effort to overcome their fear. Offer statements of positive expectation that let them know you have faith in their ability to conquer this problem. And always share the news of a successful night with other people important to your child.

In addition to social rewards, you can further encourage your children to continue in their efforts to overcome their fear with concrete rewards. You might, for example, offer to give your child a new pair of superhero PJs the first night he or she sleeps in a darkened room. Or a new flashlight or penlight to keep by their bedside might be appealing. Use anything you can afford and easily obtain that will motivate your children to stay in the dark.

Older children may be motivated to conquer their fear with a progress chart like the one on page 32. This kind of chart lets your child work toward a goal that is especially desirable. This goal may be a special toy, an afternoon at the movies, an evening out with Dad, or anything that in your child's eyes is worth working for. Each morning after your child has stayed in bed under the prescribed nighttime conditions, place one star of bravery on the chart. When the child has accumulated the agreed upon number of stars, let him or her trade them in for the reward and then, until your child is able to stay in the darkened bedroom without external motivation, make up a new chart and a new goal, and start again.

HELPFUL HINTS

The goal of this chapter has been to offer you ways to help children afraid of the dark get over that fear. While you incorporate these methods into your bedtime routine, keep these tips in mind:

• Do not use angry words or punishments to solve a fear-of-the-dark problem. If your child is not responding to the method you've chosen as easily or quickly as you would like, choose another or get professional help, but your child needs you to be always supportive and available for protection. Anger will add other fears to this nighttime problem.

• When you respond to calls in the night, don't turn the light on when you enter the room. This can reinforce your child's notion that light and comfort go together. Offer your comfort in the dark to help strengthen the association you're trying to make between darkness and security.

• Don't punish your children during the day with edicts that end, "Go to your room." Reinforce your nighttime efforts to make the bedroom a desirable place to be by reserving it for happy and peaceful times.

• If your children continue to call to you or come into your bed during the night, don't try to stop them with disciplinary tactics. Go to them, offer comfort, rehearse the coping skills, and continue your training efforts the next night.

BIBLIOTHERAPY

Who's Afraid of the Dark
Crosby Bonsall (Harper and Row, 1980)
Storm in the Night
Mary Stolz (Harper and Row, 1990)

CHAPTER 6

Fear of Things That Go Bump in the Night

If you lie perfectly still in your bed and listen carefully, you'll hear many things that go bump in the night. You may hear the house creaking as it settles, squirrels scampering across the roof, the loose siding flapping in the wind, and the wind itself whistling through the eaves and cracks. Some children, too, lie and listen to these sounds, but they hear different things; they hear bogeymen and monsters, aliens and mutant creatures, gangsters and kidnappers. They imagine that the demons are hiding somewhere in the bedroom waiting to pounce. They may be in the closet, under the bed, in a dresser drawer, or behind the curtain. Yet, if you look for them you won't see them because they move to new hiding places and sometimes they become invisible.

If your children are afraid of the monsters under their beds, no amount of logical assurances will convince them that it's safe to turn off the light and go to sleep. These children who scream for the light, clasp onto their parents and beg them to stay in the bedroom, or won't sleep in the "possessed" room at all will not get over their fear when you explain that there's nothing to be afraid of. True, the monsters are not real, but the children's fear is quite real and it won't go away if you ignore it.

WHERE NIGHT MONSTERS COME FROM

Fear of night monsters (as I'll collectively call all things that go bump in the night) is a rather common and normal occurrence among children. It was, in fact, listed as one of the top five fears facing children reported in a parent survey conducted by *Children* magazine.[1] This fear has two common roots: one in a natural developmental state where children struggle to distinguish between fantasy and reality, and the other in the anxieties of daily life.

Fantasy or Reality?

The allure of childhood often exists in the joys of an unleashed imagination. The fun of fantasy, however, is sometimes matched by a child's equally strong urge to understand and control the world. A recent study out of the University of Colorado and Brandeis University suggests that all children advance through four stages before they establish a secure boundary between what's real and what's pretend. I've listed the stages below because knowing which stage your child is in may help you pinpoint the source of the fear.

Stage One: No Boundary
Fantasy and reality are one world, and the child can't stop pretending at will.

Stage Two: Fuzzy Boundary
The child can recognize two realms but can't move from one to the other without a crutch such as costumes or toys.

Stage Three: Rigid Boundary
Child recognizes most differences between fantasy and reality and can cross the boundary easily, controlling which realm he or she is in.

Stage Four: Integrated Boundary
Child sees fantasy as a subset of reality and can be in and control both realms at once.[2]

Most three-to-five-year-olds are stuck somewhere within stages one, two, and three and so they are psychologically unable to accept your word that there are no monsters in the bedroom. For these children, the fear of things that go bump in the night grows from a normal developmental process.

Fantasy or Anxiety?

Monsters in the night may be made of more than a child's inability to draw the line between fantasy and reality. They may take on life because they give the child a concrete object to represent other fears or aggressive urges. If, for example, something upsetting is going on in the child's environment, scary monsters may appear as an expression of anxiety.

Monsters frequently invade the night's peace when children feel threatened, vulnerable, or unprotected and can't quite verbalize or understand why and don't know how to react. Going to a new school, family relocation, death, or divorce, being "replaced" by a new brother or sister, or TV and movies tales of murders, aliens, terrorists, and nuclear war are all on the list of things children worry about and which can manifest themselves as night monsters. Children can more easily express to you their fear of a fantasy monster than their fear of reality.

IGNORE OR CONFRONT?

Very often the monsters who seem to lie in bedroom closets don't stay very long. As the line between fantasy and reality becomes more clearly defined and as children learn to cope with what worries them, their complaints from the dark grow less and less intense. So, like many other childhood fears, you can wait for your children to outgrow this one. But also like most other childhood fears, there are good reasons to help your children confront their feelings now.

Using a remark like, "Oh, don't be silly. There's no such thing as monsters," may seem like an appropriate way to keep the problem from growing out of proportion, but I have found that it often backfires. Ignoring your child's fear of night monsters will probably trigger one of two reactions: (1) to avoid disappointing you or appearing "silly," the child will lie quiet, but terrified, until sleep comes and then the sleep may be restless and interrupted by nightmares; or (2) the child will scream and beg and plead until you let him or her escape the fear by sleeping on the couch or in your bedroom.

Neither response is a desirable solution. The first leaves the problem of night monsters intact and adds to it the problem of disrupted and fretful sleep. The second response does more than ignore the fear, it actually fosters it. If you let a frightened child sleep in another room "out of danger," you give the monster free reign in the child's bedroom and relay the message that there is good reason to be afraid. In addition, both cause bad habits that result in bedtime rebellion, stalling, and nightwaking when terrified children continually use every play to resist going to and staying in bed. Once your children become accustomed to sleeping on the couch or in your bed, you'll find that after the fear of monsters is long gone, they'll still be sleeping everywhere but in their own beds. The only way to rid a child's bedroom (and the world) of monsters and maintain a healthy bedtime routine is to confront the noises in the night.

Learning to confront and overcome fears is a necessary part of growing up. Although most children will outgrow their fear of things that go bump in the night, they will continue to be faced with fears throughout their lifetime. Fears like ones of public speaking, or of risk-taking, or of rejection, or of extreme heights are a part of our existence. Teaching children how to conquer the monsters in their closets will show them that they do not have to run from fears or become their victims. Instead, they have the power to face and deal with things that frighten them. The rest of this chapter will give you strategies you can use to help your children learn how to conquer this childhood fear.

BUILDING A MONSTER TRAP

A monster trap is constructed with strategies that take away a child's feelings of helplessness. The foundation is built on your assurances of protection. The structure itself is created with coping skills that keep fear in a manageable perspective, and the actual extermination mechanism is triggered by the child's newfound sense of control. The following three sections will detail how parental assurance, coping skills, and empowering strategies can be used by your child to cast out even the most fearsome night monster.

Parental Assurance

You can't use logic to assure your children that they don't need to be afraid of the things that go bump in the night. Saying "There are no such things as monsters. See . . . " as you open the closets and lift up the bedspread will only convince your children that they really do exist (or you wouldn't be wasting your time searching for them), and that they're somewhere else at the moment. You won't talk your children out of believing that their rooms have been invaded and yet it's a mistake to appease them by acknowledging that monsters really do exist. Your ultimate goal is to eliminate the fear by clarifying the line between fantasy and reality.

You can best reach this goal by accepting the fear as real and terrifying, and by acknowledging that the monsters do live in your child's imagination. Show your children that you understand their fear by offering assurances that you will always be nearby to protect them from harm and that you can teach them how to scare away the imaginary monsters. It's best to have these conversations that explore frightening feelings during the day when bedtime and monster appearances are not imminent. This gives your child the security of daylight in which to expose the fears that live in the dark.

When you talk with your children, be careful what you say. Statements like "I won't let any monsters hurt you" give validity to the existence of monsters. Instead say, "I'll always be nearby to comfort you when you're afraid." And, "I'll help you face the pretend things you're scared of so you can go to sleep without being afraid."

You can also show your children that you take their feelings seriously (without taking their monsters seriously) by taking time to talk about their fears. Sometimes children can explain exactly what form their monsters take—perhaps a shadow that the hall light casts into their room, or the way their curtains blow in the wind, or even a poster or picture on the wall. Five-year-old Timmy, for example, idolized his older brother and proudly hung a poster of his brother's favorite musical group on his bedroom wall. In the daytime, the poster made Timmy feel grown-up like his brother. But at night the musicians with their freakish makeup and hairstyles became Timmy's monsters. Once you realize the source of the fear, a few environmental changes may be all that's needed to banish the demons of the dark.

If you can not pinpoint the cause of the fear, the monster may live solely in your child's mind. In this case, a discussion of "real" and "pretend" may help your children come closer to clarifying the fuzzy distinction between the two. Role playing can help you do this. Wearing a Halloween mask, explain to your child that you are pretending to be someone else. Then take it off and show that although pretending is fun, you still are really you. Point out that TV and movie monsters are also pretend and are really people, like Mommy and Daddy, wearing masks and costumes. Let your children practice playing "pretend and real." Put the mask on them and pretend; take it off and be "real."

Reading books about nighttime monsters is another way you can talk through the problem with your child. There are several appropriate books listed at the end of this chapter that convey the child's feelings, illustrate the monsters' appearance, and show how the children can take back the night. These books will help your children talk about and face their own fears.

Coping Skills

Coping skills are the voluntary mental and physical tactics we use to help us deal with fears such as that of being alone at night (we turn on the lights and the TV), that of public speaking (we rehearse with a friendly audience), that of failure (we image ourselves in successful endeavors), or that of closed-in places (we take a deep breath and exhale slowly). These kinds of tactics help take our mind off the fearful circumstances or help us mentally change the situation to a more pleasant one. Your children can use similar tactics to help them cope with their fear of night monsters.

• *Bedtime Rituals*: Fear makes the body's adrenaline flow and causes a child to become active and anxious. You can help your child counter this bodily response by implementing calming bedtime rituals. Make sure that your children do not watch scary or stimulating TV shows the hour before bedtime. And don't let them engage in rough or overly-active play. Set aside this time for routine getting-ready-for-bed procedures like washing and changing into PJs. Then build a secure and friendly nighttime atmosphere by talking together about fun and pleasant things. Laugh, hug, and distract your children's attention away from their worries. This is not a good time to focus a conversation on your child's fear of monsters. As you yourself would not want to discuss all the reasons you're afraid of public speaking while waiting your turn to address company executives, a bedtime discussion of nighttime fears only highlights your children's anxious feelings.

Even after a calm and pleasant "Good night," your child may still resist being alone. If this happens, you can (without acknowledging that night monsters exist) grant requests to leave on the light or to sit at their bedside for awhile. It may take several weeks of using all three strategies explained in this chapter before your children are willing to face their night creatures alone, so they may need your protective presence until then. Don't, however, let your children leave the room to sleep elsewhere, and if your children still want you to stay in their bedroom after one full week of monster hunting, you may be getting stuck in a bad-habit routine rather than a protective one. In that case, review the empowering strategies explained below and choose new ones that may be more helpful to your child.

• *Protective Company*: Security blankets, pacifiers, and favorite stuffed animals help toddlers make the transition from being completely dependent on their parents for comfort to being able to comfort themselves in their new independent roles. Similarly, you can take advantage of children's ability to find support and security in imaginary friends to help them get through this developmental state. Even if your children don't have a special comforting "friend," you can offer them one now.

One mother I know helped her young son feel secure at night by helping him pile fifteen or so stuffed animals onto his bed. They were lined up and down the blanket, atop the pillow, under the sheets, and some were securely tucked under the child's arms. "Let's pretend that all these animals love you," she told her son. "And let's imagine that they are brave and strong and enjoy protecting sleeping children. Nothing can harm you when you are loved by so many good friends." This coping strategy can help children feel more secure as they attempt to confront the things that scare them in the night.

• *Other Coping Strategies*: Coping strategies such as positive self-statements, muscle relaxation, deep breathing, and positive imagery which were explained in Chapter Five may also help ease your child's reaction to fear of night monsters. However, because your children view their night monsters as real, living invaders, coping strategies alone will usually not resolve the problem. Children need to use concrete, do-something-about-it strategies to convince themselves that the demons are gone. The following will help them actively do something about their fear.

Empowering Strategies

You can not slay the dragons of the night. They live in your children's imaginations and so only your children can vanquish them. Since logical explanations about reality versus fantasy don't usually convince children that there's nothing to fear, you'll get better results if you work with their imagination rather than against it. The following strategies all put your children in charge of their imaginary world. Being in control may give them the courage they need to sleep soundly and securely.

• *Give It a Face*: Sometimes it's the *idea* of a night invader that is most terrifying to children. In this case, the fear is focused on the feelings of helplessness—not the monster itself. Often this fear can be eased by giving the monster a concrete form.

After four nights of trying to convince his five-year-old daughter, Beth, that there is nothing to be afraid of in her room, a friend of mine finally took my advice and helped his daughter actively do something about her fear. "Let's draw a picture of what the creature in your room would look like if it were real," he began. He and Beth sat down with paper, crayons, and markers, and drew a gruesome and fierce, brown monster with scales and large pointed teeth. My friend then suggested that they pretend the monster had a baby. And so Beth drew a little scaly green monster next to its mommy. Her dad commented that the mommy-monster was probably happy to have her baby nearby, so he asked Beth to draw a smiling face on the mother monster. Then, Beth and her dad created a fairy tale about a mother monster who was searching bedrooms all over the world looking for her lost baby. Then one day she found her baby in Beth's room. The mother monster was so happy to find her baby safe and sound that she jumped up and down for joy (shaking the house just a little) and gave Beth a big monster hug. Beth hung the picture in her bedroom so she would remember that the monster under her bed was just a lost baby and that the baby's mommy was now her friend.

The plan worked. Beth became delighted to have a monster in her room. Just as children can imagine horribly scary creatures, so can their imaginations turn the monster into a friend, a weakling, a protector, a baby, or anything else that gives them control of the night. Encourage your child to draw pictures, paint portraits, make clay models, and imagine pleasant, happy-ending monster stories.

• *Monster Toys*: Another concrete way to scare away nighttime fears is through daily play activities. Some parents worry that the monster-and ghost-related toys and video games their children play aggravate (if not cause) the fear of nighttime monsters. Although the viewing of very realistic horror movies and TV shows should be postponed until a child is old enough to sort out what is real and what is not (around the age of six), monster toys and video games can actually help younger children deal with their frightening aggressive urges and thoughts. Because children learn best through physical activities, monster games give children an appropriate outlet to demonstrate aggression and express scary feelings. By projecting angry and hostile behavior onto an imaginary monster, they can, in an acceptable context, begin to learn about and deal with what otherwise could become overwhelmingly fearful emotions. Don't hide all the gruesome play figures and video games your children have collected. Playing with these toys gives children a creative way to relegate their monsters to the fantasy world, express their anxieties and retain control all at the same time.[3]

• *Ghostbusting*: Many children have exorcised their nighttime monsters with daytime rituals that combine a bit of magic with a show of bravery. Emphasizing the power of pretend, you, too, can engage your child in fantasy games that rid their rooms of evil and danger.

One mother, whose six-year-old son, Todd, was terrified of the ghosts in his room and who (not coincidentally) was an avid fan of the television show "Ghostbusters," decided to use the show to help get her son over his fear. She told Todd that just as the Ghostbusters capture their ghosts in a trap, he could pretend to capture his ghosts in the vacuum cleaner. She gave him the vacuum and sent him to his bedroom to suck up the ghosts from their hiding places. Then together, they took the vacuum outside and put the bag into the garbage, tightened the lid and threw away Todd's worries.

• *Now You See It—Now You Don't*: It's difficult, even in the world of pretend, to get rid of something you've never seen. Calling on your children's imagination, ask them to draw a picture of what they think the night monster probably would look like if it were real. Once the monster is physically present on paper, your children can then imagine themselves being brave and conquering superheroes who can destroy the monster by crumpling it up and throwing it away or by burying it in the back yard. My colleague's daughter still loves to tell her friends how last summer she got rid of the space creature that was hiding in her room by folding it into a paper plane and sailing it out the door.

These adventures turn a scary situation into fun and they also give children's imagination a concrete way to get rid of their night fears.

• *Abracadabra*: The world of pretend play is a wonderful place where anything is possible. Just as the imagination can give birth to a night monster, so can it be used to cause its demise (especially for children under age six). Tell your children that in the world of make-believe, magicians have the power to make night monsters disappear. Then with as much fanfare as you like, offer your children a magic wand, teach them a magic word like "Abracadabra," and send them into the possessed room to weave a spell and turn the monster into air—POOFF!

From this same bag of tricks, many parents have been able to cleanse demon-controlled rooms with magical spray cans. Spray disinfectants and room fresheners have been known to work double duty as monster disintegrators. Let your children spray wherever they like to vaporize their fears.

• *Just in Case*: After the monsters have been banished from the bedrooms, your children may still be a bit hesitant about their powers of extermination. Some children ask to take "weapons" to bed just in case the monster returns. Play swords, toy guns, and ghost zappers can certainly be kept near the bed for emergency use. But never allow sharp objects, rope, string, or other "defenses" in the bed that could in any way hurt or become tangled around the child.

Additional, and safe, monster insurance can be offered with a flashlight. This will give your children instant light if they feel afraid and it will also allow them to double-check the monsters' hiding places to be sure they're really gone.

★ ★ ★

In each tactic suggested in this chapter you'll notice that the child is the one who seeks out and eliminates the things that go bump in the night. Although it's tempting to play the hero by bagging the bogeyman or spraying the spiders yourself, if you do it you'll further convince your children that night monsters really do exist (or there'd be no need for you to run around the room after them), and then your children will soon be calling in the night, "They're back!" Remember: the monsters belong to your children; they must conquer them by themselves in order to banish their fears to the by-gone years of childhood.

BIBLIOTHERAPY

Harry and the Terrible Whatzit
Dick Gackenbach (Clarion, 1979)

My Mama Says There Aren't Any Zombies, Ghosts, Vampires, Creatures, Demons, Monsters, Fiends, Goblins, or Things
Judith Viorst (Aladdin Books, 1988)

The Monster at the End of the Book
Jon Stone (Golden—A Sesame Street Book, 1977)

The Monster Is Coming

Michaela Morgan and Sue Porter (Harper & Row, 1988)

What's Under My Bed?
James Stevenson (Willow, 1990)

Where the Wild Things Are
Maurice Sendak (Harper & Row, 1963)

CHAPTER 7

Separation Anxiety

Some children think of sleep as a scary place that takes them away from their parents. These children who are afraid to go to sleep alone are often suffering from separation anxiety—the intense emotional distress some feel when shut off from their parents for any length of time. Because they panic at the thought of being left alone at bedtime, they cry and plead, "Please, sleep with me." Or, "I want to sleep in your room." Or, "Don't leave me! Let me stay in the living room with you." As we all know, in some cases, children cry out simply because they don't want to go to bed, but in other cases the fear of separation is quite real and the panic response is not meant to be manipulative; it is a cry for help.

REBELLION OR FEAR?

Children do not suddenly develop separation anxiety at bedtime. If otherwise independent children, who easily separate from their parents during the day, willingly go to school or barely give a nodding good-bye when being left with a sitter, cry out, "Don't leave me. Stay with me," when you try to put them to bed, the problem is in faulty bedtime habits that you've both developed. Solutions for these kinds of bedtime problems are offered in Part One.

On the other hand, if during the day your children cling to you, cry if your leave them with a sitter, and scream when you leave them at school, and then also act fearful and cry when you try to put them to bed, the problem is most likely related to separation anxiety.

WHY IT HURTS TO BE APART

There are two most common reasons children experience separation anxiety when parted from their parents: one is rooted in the normal developmental process of becoming independent and the other is related to the way parents react to a child's fear of separation.

Just a Stage

Sometime between six and twelve months, all mentally healthy children become aware of their parents as separate individuals and begin to express displeasure when the parent leaves. This period called separation protest is a normal developmental stage that occurs because babies begin to realize that being separate involves some danger and also because at this stage babies don't perceive object permanence and so can't imagine where you are if you're not in sight. When you leave it appears that you're gone forever.

Children experience the distress of this anxiety in varying degrees. Most will cry for only a short while and then calm down and play happily. Some will cry inconsolably until the parent returns. Some will protest only when left in unfamiliar surroundings; others will cry even when left with grandparents in their own homes. And still others will confound their parents by contentedly staying with a sitter one day, and screaming in horror the next.

The duration of separation fear is also variable. Some babies quickly outgrow it and yet some five-year-olds still resist being separated from their parents. Others grow out of this stage and then regress when something new or frightening happens: the first day on the school bus, a new sibling, or a traumatic life change like a family death or divorce.

In this developmental stage the intensity and duration of separation fear is innately unique to each child. But in the majority of cases, the separation protests subside within a half hour after the parents leave. This is perfectly normal and should not be viewed as an indication that the chid is having emotional difficulties. If, however, a child does not calm down until the parent returns, and appears truly panicked for long time periods, then he or she is probably experiencing more than normal developmental fears and will need help to overcome this anxiety. As explained in the next section, intense separation anxiety is often fostered by the parents' response to the initial separation protests.

Encouraged Dependence

Children's refusal to be left alone at bedtime is often the result of the way their parents reacted to infantile separation anxiety. Although separation protest is a normal developmental stage, parents sometimes respond to the fear in oversolicitous ways that encourage intense separation anxiety. For example, one day nine-month-old Kevin screamed when his mom left him at the usual time with a neighborhood sitter while she went food shopping. Rather than upset him again, his mom decided to take Kevin with her in the future and explained to the baby-sitter that he wouldn't be coming for his weekly visit anymore. Similarly, Susanne gave up her daily one-mile run because her eighteen-month-old daughter (who was left during this time in the care of her father) cried so pitifully every time Susanne went to the closet for her running shoes. And Debbie and Sean agreed to drop out of their bowling league because their two-year-old became so upset everytime they left.

These children cried because they were afraid their parents wouldn't return. Because their parents tried to ease their fears by not leaving at all, the children were denied the opportunity to learn that when parents leave, they always come back. If they don't learn that parents must sometimes leave their children, and that they can calm and soothe themselves, and that they are safe even when separated from their parents, then they will fear the separation that bedtime brings. In these cases, the children's anxieties were encouraged by their parents' attempts to prevent their fears.

In other cases, I have seen children cling to their parents because they have learned from their parents that independence is a dangerous thing. Overly protective parents have their own brand of separation anxiety. They hover over toddlers with stern warnings like, "Be careful. You're going to fall. Hold on." They respond to adventurous feats like trying to tumblesault with reprimands like, "Don't do that. You're going to hurt yourself!" And they say good-bye before even the shortest separation with sad faces, worried expressions, desperate hugs and kisses, and a litany of I'm-going-to-miss-yous. In these cases the parents' fear of the child's growing independence is passed on to their children who then worry at bedtime that sleep too is dangerous without their parents' protection.

The bottom line on bedtime separation anxiety is that for a variety of reasons, some children are genuinely afraid to go to bed by themselves. Knowing why your children are experiencing this fear will help you understand why some solutions aggravate the problem and others will solve it.

THE WRONG WAY TO CALM THE CRIES

The whining and clinging and crying of children experiencing separation anxiety can be quite irritating. After a long day of dealing with a child who won't let you leave his side, you may get angry when he or she persists in crying for you at night also. It's understandable why you might finally say, "I've catered to your demands all day, but now I want some time to myself, so cry if your want, but I'm saying good night and closing this door." Although understandable, this solution will increase rather than end the child's fears.

Some parents accuse a child pulling nighttime tantrums of being "a baby" or "spoiled." They follow up these accusations with actions or punishments like spankings, restriction of privileges, or angry words that they hope will force the child to grow up and learn how to behave. Although various modes of discipline will stop bedtime tantrums caused by general resistance or rebellion, they can not stop the cries of children truly panicked by the fear of separation. Angry responses, punishments, and belittling remarks are the wrong way to address bedtime separation problems.

On the other end of the reaction spectrum, some parents offer too much comfort to children experiencing separation anxiety. Obviously, the easiest way to calm the night cries is to avoid separation at all. Lisa calms her son's fears by lying down in his bed with him every night until he falls asleep. With the same good intentions, Gary and Nicole let their daughter fall asleep on the living room couch while they watch TV. But when these children wake in the middle of the night and find themselves alone, they run to their parents' bed and sleep there for the rest of the night. These "remedies" calm the cries, but they don't solve the problem. Children experiencing intense separation anxiety need to learn how to be apart from their parents. Giving into their fears further enforces their belief that they can not function unless attached to you.

BETTER WAYS TO EASE THE FEAR

Whether your children's separation anxiety occurs as a developmental stage or as a learned behavior, you can teach them how to accept nighttime separation as a natural and painless part of each day. Because the problem is not solely a nighttime one, you'll be most successful in your efforts if you help your children deal with both their daytime and nighttime fears; this will assure them of their ability to survive and even thrive without you nearby.

Daytime Strategies
Practice makes perfect. In other areas of child development I'm sure you've realized that the best way to learn any new skill like walking, talking, or clapping hands is through repetitive trials. Sometimes the effort is successful; other times it fails but eventually, with practice, you watch your children succeed and advance in growth, development, and confidence. The skill of separation is learned in the same way.

In order for children to overcome their fear of separation, they need opportunities to practice being away from you and to experience your return. At first they may bring your children to tears, but that's part of the learning process. As parents we cannot (and should not try to) shelter our children from all frustration and disappointment; life will not be as kind. If your children scream every time you lock yourself in the bathroom for a few moments of privacy, don't open the door to stop the crying. Let your children learn that during your absence nothing awful happens and that you do return. If your children protest when you're about to go out for a while by yourself, don't change your plans just to stop the noise. Go; give your children another chance to practice being without you, and then see you come back.

Even when you're together you and your children can rehearse separation. Send your child to fetch something in another room. Leave the room yourself for a few minutes (or seconds), and praise your children for staying alone while you were gone. Small children can learn about separation through games like peekaboo and hide-and-seek. The goal is to repeatedly experience situations that prove to your children that when you go away they are safe and you do always return.

If your children go to day-care or school, they have scheduled opportunities to practice the skills of separation. If not, you'll need to create occasions for separation by leaving your children with a familiar person several times each week while you shop or simply walk around the block. Whenever you leave your children always follow these separation rules:

• *Stay calm:* Emotions are contagious so display the feelings you want your children to catch. Don't fret and worry, or look anxious or hesitant. Remain cheerful; smile, and with confidence say "Good-bye." No matter how loudly your children scream and beg, keep smiling.

• *Don't drag out your good-byes*: Explain to your child that you're going out and will return. You might want to stick around for a while to make sure that she's well acquainted with the sitter, teacher, and/or surroundings. Try to involve her in an activity. But once you decide it's time to leave, give your child a few minutes warning. Smile; say your cheerful good-byes and then leave. Don't drag out your departure with one more kiss and another assurance of your love. Don't get to the door and then come back to calm the cries. This encourages your child to believe that if she cries hard enough you might change your mind.

• *Don't discourage tears*: It is unreasonable to ask your children to stop crying or to be brave. Let them cry. It's their way of expressing how they feel and your opportunity to offer your understanding. Saying, "I know you feel sad when I leave, but I must go and I'll be back at suppertime," assures children that you aren't ignoring or misinterpreting their feelings and it helps them accept the separation as inevitable.

• *Never sneak out:* It is very tempting to dodge out the back door when your children are distracted for a moment—but don't do it. Eventually, children will notice your disappearance, but then they have no way of knowing that they haven't been abandoned forever. Always be honest and direct. Say "Good-bye," assure that you will return, and then leave.

• *Return when promised:* Don't tell children, "I'll be right back," and then go out for two hours. When dealing with separation anxieties, it's important that your children learn to trust you. If you'll be gone until dark, say so. If you're going to be late, call on the phone and explain. Being honest about all the details of your departure and return makes it easier for your children to believe your promise that the separation is temporary and safe.

• *Return with a smile:* When you return, your children (who probably have been quite content while you were gone) may burst into tears, run to your arms, and cling to you for dear life. Or, they may completely ignore you. Either response is perfectly normal, but you should continue teaching the lesson of separation by remaining cheerful and calm. A parent who gets teary and insists, "I missed you so much. Are you okay? Did you miss me?" teaches the child that there really is danger in being alone.

• *Nighttime Strategies:* Nighttime strategies to end separation anxiety are a bit more difficult to practice than daytime ones. This is because after you say "Good-bye" during the day, you can leave and get away from the crying, and your child has no choice but to eventually accept your absence. At nighttime, however, after you say "Good night" you're still physically present in the house and so you can't escape the crying and your child will persist in screaming for you or even in following you around. So, in addition to practicing the daytime tactics explained above, desensitization at bedtime is the best way to end nighttime separation fears.

Desensitization is a method of gradual, psychological adjustment that allows a fearful person to *slowly* master the fear and cope with the circumstances causing the fear. Like the steps listed previously for overcoming fear of the dark which involve gradually lowering the amount of light in the room, the goal of using this method to deal with separation anxiety is gradually to put greater and greater physical distance between you and your child until the child no longer needs your presence to drift off to sleep.

An hour or so before bedtime, explain to your children that you know they can learn to sleep alone now because they're getting so grown up and that starting that night you're going to help them do it. Keep a cheerful and optimistic attitude throughout the conversation and repeat the positive expectations for success. If you know you're going to face resistance, you can build motivation into the plan by offering a special reward for cooperation. (See page 27 for a complete discussion of positive incentives.)

Throughout the process always offer encouragement each night and praise the following morning, and follow these four steps:

• *Step 1:* Examine the status quo. How do your children fall asleep right now? Each progressive step in the desensitization process will move away from this point.

• *Step 2:* Put greater physical distance between you and your child than is presently the case as found in Step 1.

> If your child usually sleeps in your bed, put a cot or a soft bed of blankets next to your bed. Your child may sleep there by himself but will still have your nearby.

> If your child usually sleeps near you on the couch in the living room, make up a soft bed on the floor away from you and the couch.

> If you sleep next to your child in his bed until he falls asleep, sit up on the bed without making physical contact.

If you usually sit on your child's bed, now sit in a nearby chair.

As you move one step away from the usual bedtime routine follow these guidelines: (1) Try not to move backward; once you've established the new sleeping arrangement, don't readily give in and resume old habits. (2) Offer statements of positive expectations. Let your child know that you don't expect to stay nearby for much longer because you know that eventually he won't need your help to get to sleep. (3) If, during the night, your child calls out or tries to sneak back into the living room or into your bed, calmly but firmly reestablish the getting-to-sleep positions used at bedtime.

Once your child successfully falls asleep under the new conditions for three consecutive nights, move on to Step 3.

• *Step 3:* Move one step further away from your child at bedtime. The usual sequence of moves pushes the child from the parents' bed or the couch to a nearby bed of blankets on the floor. Then the child moves to his own bed but with the parent sitting on the edge to provide security until the child falls asleep. Then the parent moves to a chair by the child's bedside where there is no physical contact.

Once you say "Good night" all pleasantries should stop. Don't chat with your child; don't rub his back or offer more hugs and kisses. This is time for sleep. Also remember to keep moving further apart; repeat the positive message that soon you child won't need your help to sleep, and always reestablish bedtime positions if your child calls out or leaves his bed in the middle of the night.

• *Step 4:* Continue moving further and further away in three-night intervals—outside the door, down the hall, down the stairs. Once you've moved out of sight, don't go back. If your child calls out for you, don't return to the room; just call back, "I'm right here. Go to sleep." Use a firm and confident, yet calm, voice. Don't yell or get angry; just let your child know that if he doesn't stay in bed, then you won't sit there. If your child should get out of bed, leave your post and go to another part of the house until he gets back into bed; then return. Be consistent on this point.

Once you've moved out of the bedroom, your child is well on his way to conquering his fear of separation and it may then take firm enforcement of limits to break the habit of having you in sight. Make sure your child knows that if he gets out of bed, you're gone.

You can also encourage cooperation with positive incentives. Marge, for example, found that her son, Tad, was agreeable to the separation process until she moved her chair into the hall out of his sight. Then the crying began again. To help him continue the desensitization process, Marge made up a progress chart like the one on page 32. Then she bought several small toys at the local dime store, wrapped each one in brightly colored paper and put them in what she called the Reward Box. Each morning after Tad successfully fell asleep with his mom out of the room, he was praised and allowed to paste one sticker on his chart. When he had three stickers in a row, he was allowed to take one surprise gift out of the box. Then that night, his mom moved one step further away and Tad began his sticker collection again. "It turned the separation process into a game," Marge said, "and the five dollars I spent on the little gifts was worth every penny considering that it helped Tad happily give up his need to have me at his side all night."

In addition to desensitization, firm limits, praise, and rewards, you can support your children's efforts to let go of their fears with these helpers:

• *Routines:* Children who suffer separation anxiety are especially vulnerable to abrupt or unpredictable changes in their schedules. You can help your children accept your gradual separation by establishing a bedtime routine; routines that are consistent and predictable give children a sense of safety and security. At the same time every night, begin a ritual of washing and changing and add a bedtime story or evening prayer if you like. Reserve some time for tucking in and quiet talk and then say "Good night." When you follow the same preparatory steps every night at the same time, your children know what to expect and this helps ease their fears.

• *Substitute objects:* Infants and toddlers often become attached to what we sometimes call "lovies." These teddy bears, blankets, pacifiers, etc., help children cope with the transition from being dependent on their parents for comfort to learning how to comfort themselves. With this philosophy in mind, offer your children some object of yours that will give them comfort without direct physical contact with you. This object may be a scarf dabbed in your perfume or aftershave, or a sweatshirt you often wear, or even one of your pajama tops. Holding on tightly to something of yours will help your children cope with their fears of abandonment.

• *Self-talk:* Encourage your school age children to say brave and comforting statements to themselves whenever they feel lonely or fearful. Statements like, "I miss my mommy, but I know she's nearby if I need her," help children remember that they are not really alone. And statements like, "I'm proud of myself for being grown-up enough to sleep by myself now," will motivate children to want to sleep alone. Practice positive self-talk over and over again during the day and right before bedtime so that when the worries begin, your children can easily remember the positive things they can say to make themselves feel better.

WHY BOTHER?

These coping strategies along with the desensitization process will break the ties that are keeping your children from functioning independently. Although when used consistently they *will* work, many parents ask me, "Why should I bother to use this process to end a natural developmental stage if doing it takes away my own personal time at night and robs me of sleep when I have to do it again in the middle of the night?" The answer I always give focuses on what's best for children in the long run. Separation anxiety is a natural stage of child development, but if the child is coddled and protected from dealing with the fear of separation, the fear grows; as long as this fear persists it is difficult for the child to grow to be independent and self-sufficient. In fact the ability of young children to deal successfully with their fears of separation allows them to become teenagers who are capable of making close friends, adults who can love their spouses, and parents who can nurture their own children to independence. That's why it's important to help your children get over their fear of separation.

WHAT'S WRONG WITH THIS PICTURE?

As parents we wouldn't intentionally keep our children habitually fearful of separation; we do it unknowingly as we grapple with the young cries that say, "Don't leave me." As you read through the following typical scene of separation fears and remedies, watch for the pitfalls that are making the separation process more complex and difficult for this parent and child.

Since Kaitlyn's birth three years ago, Janice has been a stay-at-home mom. Now she and her husband have agreed that it's time to put Kaitlyn in preschool while Janice goes back to part-time work. Knowing Kaitlyn is very attached to her, Janice expected that her daughter might cry at first when it was time to leave her at the school, but she didn't expect her to cry so pitifully nor to feel so guilty about it herself.

On that first day, Kaitlyn did cry and run after her mother trying to leave the preschool. No matter how Janice tried to console her, Kaitlyn wouldn't calm down or listen to reason. Eventually, the teacher had to pry Kaitlyn from Janice's leg and carry her kicking and squirming body back into the classroom.

Janice cried all the way to work.

When she returned that afternoon, Janice found Kaitlyn sitting comfortably next to her teacher listening to a story. But when Kaitlyn saw Janice at the door, the little girl ran to her in a burst of tears. Janice dropped to her knees and tearfully hugged and kissed her daughter. "It's all right now. I'm back," she whispered. "I missed you too but I'm back now. Let's go home." Then like the white knight rescuing the damsel in distress, Janice picked up Kaitlyn in her arms and carried her to he car.

That night Kaitlyn threw a tantrum at bedtime. Although she usually went to sleep without trouble, this night she cried for her mom to stay by her bedside. Still feeling guilty about leaving Kaitlyn during the day, Janice didn't want to upset her daughter again at night. And so Janice lay down in Kaitlyn's bed and held her daughter close until she fell asleep.

The next morning, Kaitlyn again cried when she arrived at the preschool. Janice stayed for awhile to help her adjust slowly to the separation and the teacher skillfully engaged Kaitlyn in a fun activity to distract her from her fear. When Janice saw her daughter contentedly playing with blocks, she quickly left before Kaitlyn could start crying. Because Janice didn't have to go through the crying scene again, she felt happier about the arrangement as she drove to work. She didn't know of course that when Kaitlyn realized her mother was gone, her crying was longer and more intense than it had been the day before. When Janice returned, she and Kaitlyn repeated the anxious and tearful reunion of the day before.

That night and the next and the next, Kaitlyn would again cry for her mother to lie with her and Janice would again feel guilty about saying no. The pattern of dependency was set.

Children can't become independent beings when they experience trickery, emotionally upsetting separation and reunion scenes, and continued appeasement. They need honest explanations and experiences to teach them that parents and children can not always be together, but when apart they both can feel happy and confident and they will always come back together again. When your children learn these lessons, they will welcome sleep without fear.

BIBLIOTHERAPY

Leaving Home
Arlene Richards (Atheneum, 1980)

Maybe She Forgot
Ellen Kandoian (Cobblehill, 1990)

The Goodbye Book
Judith Viorst (Atheneum, 1988)

The Goodbye Painting
Linda Berman (Human Sciences Press, 1983)

CHAPTER 8

Nightmares

Is there anyone of us who can't relate to the word *nightmare*? Because we've all experienced this nocturnal chiller, we can readily define it as a dream that evokes deep emotions like anxiety, fear, anger, aggression, grief and loss, and from which we wake startled and frightened. Still, despite our familiarity with nightmares (or perhaps because of them), as parents we worry about the causes of and remedies for the nightmares that disturb the slumber of our children.

We can better deal with our children's nightmares if we first understand them. This chapter will explain how the quality and content of dreams change with age, why children have nightmares more frequently than adults, what causes the terror, and how we can ease the fear.

A CHILD'S SLEEP

Dreams occur in one particular level of sleep known as rapid eye movement (REM) sleep. This stage takes place four or five times during the nightly sleep cycle and is apparent in the way our eyes move under their lids and we lie very still. During REM sleep, breathing and heart rate become irregular and nerve messages to the limbs are blocked within the spinal cord.

While the body is paralyzed in this way, the brain is awake and gives life to our dreams.

Infants spend almost eighty percent of their sleep time in REM periods; that proportion then gradually dwindles to merely twenty-five percent in adults. This difference in the length of REM periods gives children more opportunity to experience nightmares—children have nightmares ten times more frequently than middle-aged people. And so it is the very structure of children's sleep patterns that can make them prone to nightmares.

A CHILD'S DREAMS

Dream researchers have discovered very specific details about children's dreams and nightmares. They have found that a child's mental processes in sleep are not more sophisticated than when he is awake, and children dream about the same sort of things they talk about during the day. Dreams typical in two- to eight-year-olds are as follows:

- *Two-year-olds:* The dream world of two-year-olds is a nondescript, one-dimensional place of vague settings. It holds static images of things like houses and animals seen during the day. There is very little drama or social interaction occurring in the dreams.
- *Three-to four-year-olds:* Three-and four-year-olds often dream of animals rather family members. The action of their dreams usually focuses on daily functions such as eating or drinking. They begin to experience the most common nightmare plot of being chased and frightened by non-human forms. Because these children can't yet draw the line between what's real and what's fantasy in their lives and can't fully verbalize their feelings, their dreams take on a terrorizing dimension that can't always be quickly erased when they are awakened. Some perfectly healthy preschoolers have nightmares several times a month. Studies have found that the number and intensity of nightmares often peak between ages four-and-a-half to five.

- *Five-and six-year-olds:* As children become more concrete in their thinking skills the storylines of their dreams become more complex. The animals of their dreams dress and behave as people. There is interaction between characters and recreation and play are dominant themes. The faces of strangers appear and the monsters of earlier dreams turn into bad guys, kidnappers, and thugs.
- *Seven-and eight-year-olds:* The dreams of older children grow in complexity and contain plots and subplots, most of which focus on real-life concerns in which the dreamer takes an active part. The content of the dreams is highly personal and focuses more often on family and friends than on animals.

Whatever your child's age, when a nightmare strikes you'll most naturally want to know, "What's causing this?" The next section will give you some insight into the roots of children's bad dreams.

CAUSES OF NIGHTMARES

Through the years I have found that most nightmares have no deep-seated psychological origin and are not necessarily a cause for concern. The dreams which wake your children and bring them to horrifying screams in the night may be outlets for normal emotional concerns of development. The source of children's concerns are everywhere about them every day.

Internal Sources

As children grow and venture away from their parents, they begin to experience unfamiliar and frightening feelings. A two-year-old struggling with toilet training may for the first time feel shame and embarrassment. A three-year-old who suddenly feels aggressive toward friends may become frightened by these hostile impulses. Many children try to hide their feelings of anger and jealousy at the arrival of a new sibling. Not knowing exactly what they feel or why, or even how to verbally express themselves, children will project their confusion into their dreams as frightening monsters. In these cases, it's their own budding and natural impulses that terrify young children in the night.

I recall the nightmares of a five-year-old boy named Derek who was a chronic bedwetter. Every night, Derek dreamed he was being chased by a giant elephant who kept squirting him with water from his trunk. Derek would wake crying hysterically and shouting, "Stop it! Stop it! I don't want to get wet!" As you might guess, Derek would wake with his bed and pajamas soaked with urine. He would try to explain to his parents that the elephant got him wet, but all they knew for sure was that once again they were losing sleep to change Derek's clothing and bed sheets.

External Sources

It would seem that horror movies, war epics, superheroes, and villains are the things that nightmares are made of. Research shows, however, that the terrifying images of the media rarely, in themselves, trigger nightmares. But they can uncover hidden fears and cause nightmares in children already anxious about being harmed.

Children's hidden fears frequently have their roots in real-life traumatic events. A neighborhood bully, for example, may activate dreams of being chased. A family divorce or death may evolve into dreams of abandonment. And an insensitive teacher may spark dreams of being lost or climbing unconquerable mountains.

Four-year-old Jessica, for example, woke at four in the morning screaming for her mother to save her. Through choking tears she told her parents that a big fish was chasing her. Neither Jessica or her mother remembered that the day before Jessica had seen dead fish lined up at the market. What seemed inconsequential in the daylight came back at night begging for understanding.

Physical Sources

Occasionally, frightened nightwakings grow from purely physical sources. Any respiratory problem caused by factors such as allergies, head colds, or the flu can interfere with a child's breathing and bring on bad dreams. Pain from broken bones, stitches, wounds, or any other source also can trigger fearful images in the night. Pediatricians are also familiar with patients who wake in the night with very high fevers (usually over 103 degrees) and have hallucinations. For days or even weeks after the fever passes, these children may have nightmares that express their fear of the hallucinogenic experience.

Personality

Although most children over the age of two experience nightmares, they may become more troublesome for children of certain personalities. Children like eight-year-old Kate, for example, tend to keep their feelings bottled up inside. Kate was the pitcher on the girl's softball team and was admired for her ability to stay calm and cool under pressure. Her parents knew, however, that Kate's doubts and fears found their release in occasional nightmares.

Other children find it difficult to adjust to new or different situations. Children, like three-year-old Raymond, incessantly worry about every change in the daily schedule and so face more tense moments in their day. Raymond's fear of uncertainty wakes him in the middle of the night three to four times a month.

You may also find that if your children are particularly sensitive or imaginative, they are susceptible to nightmares. These children may brood over even the most casual negative comment or may have difficulty seeing that line between fantasy and reality. Their impressionable nature and unbounded perceptions are likely to result in anxiety dreams. You should keep these individual differences in mind when you're tempted to compare the frequency of nightmares among siblings and friends.

SOLUTIONS

There is no need to become too concerned when children cry out in the night as they awaken from a nightmare. But of course you can't just roll over and ignore the cries either. Most nightmare experiences are best handled by letting your children know that you're there to protect and comfort them and that in the light of day you can help them learn to understand and manage their land of dreams.

Offer Comfort

Go quickly to your children when they call out in frightened cries, but don't dash in turning on the lights and making a ruckus. Your children may be only half awake and will fall back to sleep more easily if you don't arouse them; you also don't want to build the association between light and safety that causes children to become fearful of the dark. Turn on the hall light or a night-light and then calmly hold or hug them, offer sympathy, and support that focuses on their fear—not the dream.

Although you and I know that it was "only a dream" and that no one is chasing the child, he or she is rarely comforted by these facts. Instead, assure the child by saying, "You must feel terribly frightened." Or, "I understand; I've had bad dreams too." Talk in a calm, soothing way and assure your children that you are nearby and will not let anything bad happen. Often your gentle voice and mere presence are all that are needed to help your children fall back to sleep.

If your children appear wide-awake, you might calm them by repeating some of their usual bedtime ritual. This brings them back to reality and sets up the reassuring normalcy of sleep. Take them to the bathroom, read a story, offer a drink, and then tuck them in again. If your children want to talk about their dream, listen intently and sympathize with their feelings. Hold your comments and explanations until the next day when, if your children want to continue the conversation, they will be fully awake, calmer and reassured.

Give Control

Sometimes nightmares seem so real to children that the memory of the fear lingers. This can cause a vicious cycle that actually encourages nightmares because the child goes to sleep fretting that the dream will return and this anxiety releases itself in the dreaded bad dreams. In this case, because nightmares are especially scary in the way they make us feel helpless, giving your child control over bad dreams can ease their impact.

If your children are afraid to go to sleep because they fear nightmares, work with these fears in the daytime. Begin by simply talking. Ask your children to describe the dreams; if they can't remember details, ask them to try to explain how they feel when they have the dream. Following the example of the Senoi Indians of Malaysia you can then use your child's imagination in a playful way to rewrite the script in the next night's dream.

The Senois explain that since a nightmare is a story you make up, if you don't like the outcome you can change it. Emphasizing that the nighttime monsters aren't real but are pretend characters the imagination invents, suggest to your children that they imagine themselves confronting the scary night intruder and chasing it away. Or, you might retell the dream with an ending in which your child and the "monster" make friends by playing a favorite game. You might also suggest that your children bring "dream helpers" into their night stories. These helpers may be parents, friends, teachers, superheroes, etc., who have special powers to erase the danger and protect the child. The power of positive suggestion can take away the helpless feelings and may eliminate the nightmares completely or ease the child's fearful reaction to them.

You can take this rewriting method a step further by encouraging your children to draw pictures of their nightmares. This puts the dreamer in charge because once the night stalker is down on paper it loses power to do harm. Now your children can add details to the scene that will make it more comforting and controllable. Help them draw in their dream helpers and add happy faces to the evil doers and the dreamer.

As you rework the scene, encourage your children to look for solutions themselves. The following questions, adapted from the book, *Nightmare Help*, can be used to guide your children in their efforts to gain control of the night.

Questions to Ask Myself

After you and your child draw a dream picture, help him
or her answer the following questions:

1. How do I feel when I look at this dream picture?
2. How can I make myself feel safe enough to reenter this
   scary dream?
3. If I use my imagination, can I create a solution that will
   help?
4. If I feel helpless, who can help me?

Questions to Ask the Monster

1. Why have you come to scare me?
2. What do you want?
3. If I stop running away, can we talk?
4. If you could talk, what would you say?
5. What's good about you?
6. Do you have any children?
7. Can we be friends?*

This exploration gives your child control of the danger and it
also turns the feelings of fear and helplessness into an adventurous and enjoyable game.

General Guidelines

As you go with your child into this realm of the night, keep the
following guidelines in mind:

• Don't blow the nightmare problem out of proportion. Most
children will experience this night fear, fall back to sleep, and
live happily until the next midnight adventure. Deal with your
child's immediate fear through sympathy and comfort and then
drop it unless the fear continues the following day.

• Don't try to analyze the origins of the nightmares. It's
tempting to look for hidden meaning in the dreams or insight
into your child's soul through these night "messages." However, digging and delving is likely to arouse your child's fears

---

*From *Nightmare Help* © 1986, 1989 by Anne Sayre Wiseman. Reprinted
by permission of Ten Speed Press, Berkeley, California.

and convey that there really is something abnormal or dangerous about these dreams. Unless the nightmares fall into the "serious" category as explained below, deal with your child's feelings about the dreams rather than the dreams themselves.

• Don't lie down in your children's bed or take them to your
bed when they cry out in fear. Because nightmares are a normal,
developmental, and recurring part of childhood, you don't want
to give your children the message that they are a cause to break
nighttime rules. Sit next to your children, hold their hands, give
them the security of your presence, but don't become the white
knight who alone has the power to shield them from harm. Staying in their own beds gives children opportunity to learn how to
cope with their fears rather than feel that they're incapable of
protecting themselves. If your children come to believe that
only your continued presence throughout the night can ward off
the nightmares, then you've set up a subtle form of reinforcement that can cause continuous nightmares.

• Don't hesitate to acknowledge your children's fears. Some
parents believe they can lessen the fear by underplaying its seri-
ousness. Although there's no reason to overreact, your children
need to know that you understand their feelings and accept
them as valid. If you refuse to do that, your children may stop
talking about their bad dreams and the fears will grow. Remember, instead of saying, "There's nothing to be scared about,"
say, "You seem to feel very scared."

PREVENTION

You can't completely prevent your children's nightmares because they're a normal developmental experience. You can,
however, lessen the severity of some internal and external factors that are known to build tension in children and cause nightmares. To begin, keep the following suggestions in mind.

Create Bedtime Rituals
Once again, calm bedtime rituals are a helpful way to ease the
tensions of the day and send children off to a sound sleep. The
predictability of nightly routines gives children a sense of con-

trol that eases the helpless feeling common in nightmares. The quiet period before sleep gives children a physical and mental space to unwind and approach sleep relaxed and unstressed. See page 9 for a full discussion of bedtime rituals.

Schedule Daily Talks

Because nightmares are often rooted in everyday tensions, you can ease the stress of growing up by scheduling time for daily talks. Encourage your children to talk freely about how they feel. Too often our conversations stay on the surface level and discuss only the details of "what we did today." Children then push their feelings about their activities deep into those places in the mind that seek release at night. Getting worries, hostilities, and fears out into the open is wonderful preventative therapy for nightmares and gives you the added bonus of developing an honest and open relationship with your children.

Prepare for New Experiences

Uncertainty breeds fear. You can help ease your children's daily tensions by taking time to prepare them for new experiences. Knowing their children will cry if told in advance that something new or different is on the day's agenda, some parents withhold information until the last minute. Others of us simply get caught up in busy schedules and wisk our children from one new experience to another without time for discussion. Fear of the unknown is real in all of us; help your children adjust to new experiences by giving them explanations, time and patience.

Arrange Exercise Opportunities

You can also help ease day-to-day tensions with exercise because children need opportunities to work off excess tension. The way they usually run, jump, hop, and race through each day gives you some idea how intense is their need to get rid of built-up energy. If your children are going through a stage of frequent nightmares, be sure that their physical need for action is met each day; ironically, it just may be what they need to calm down.

Monitor TV Viewing

Although studies have shown that most often horrors of the media don't directly cause nightmares, we do know that they up-root fears that may be already present in the child. It's wise then to choose age-appropriate programs for your children (remem-bering that before the age of five, they have great difficulty dis-tinguishing between reality and fantasy). As part of the calming bedtime routine, you should restrict all horror movies or violent TV shows in the hour before bedtime.

Allow Security Objects

As children get older we sometimes become embarrassed by their tattered security objects. We may even worry that a child's attachment to "baby" items like blankets, teddy bears, or paci-fiers indicates a lack of emotional maturity and growth. Don't worry and don't take them away from your children at night. Although you may certainly restrict their use at school, or church, or during outdoor play, freely encourage their use at night. These security objects give your children a transitional hold on something physical that offers them courage and com-fort without calling to you. As they struggle to leave your pro-tective arms and find ways to calm their own fears, security ob-jects are an "emotionally mature" way to leap toward independence.

MORE SERIOUS NIGHTMARE PROBLEMS

In the vast majority of cases, children's nightmares only occa-sionally disrupt the night and are best handled with emphasis on the feelings evoked by the dreams rather than the dreams them-selves. However, sometimes the nightmare problem can become so frequent and/or intense that it requires more careful examina-tion. If your child has nightmares three to five times a week for more than a month or frequently experiences frightening dreams with a recurrent theme, the dreams may be a warning signal of your child's struggle to deal with a specific daytime problem. In this case I suggest that you try to use the content of the nightmare to help your child overcome the difficulty.

Begin your exploration of frequent nightmares by scheduling daily conversation time with your children. Many children will quickly reveal what's on their mind if given the opportunity to talk freely. But again, because it's best not to show too much concern, don't ask probing questions or try to psychoanalyze every aspect of the dream. Let your children do the talking. Encourage them to talk about their dreams and ask them if they can think of any way in which the dream is like their daily life. Ask questions like:

- What is it about the dream that scares you the most?
- What is it at school or home that scares you the most?
- If you could change one thing about your dream, what would it be?
- If you could change one thing about your day, what would it be?

If your child can't immediately pinpoint the problem, continue to offer comfort and sympathy and keep talking. The opportunity to talk with and confide in a sympathetic person is the core of nightmare therapy.

If your child does reveal a secret fear, encourage more communication. Very often the mere verbalization of the problem is enough to unburden the child. Putting the fearful feelings into words and sharing stored-up anxieties takes them out of the realm of darkness and puts them in a light that's manageable and controllable.

If talking about the problem doesn't end the nightmares, you and your child should do something concrete to ease the problem. John, for example, decided to do something specific about his son's daytime fear when he realized it was the cause of a frequent nightmare. In the recurring dream a man dressed all in black kept following his son, Keith, down the hallways of the school. Every time Keith came near the door, the man appeared and blocked his way. Keith felt terrified because he couldn't get out of the school to go home. After drawing a picture of the man and talking to his son about the dream, John found out that Keith was afraid of the schoolyard bully who had been teasing him every day for about a month. Although John was tempted to assure his son with a simplistic, "Oh, don't worry about him; he won't really hurt anybody," John decided to do something to help Keith cope with the fear. John phoned his son's teacher, explained his concern about the bully and asked for more careful supervision of playtime and dismissal time. Although Keith was never in any real danger, the feeling of having a protective helper in his teacher eased his fears and the nightmares ceased.

In another case, a kindergartner named Sue dreamed continually about a smelly skunk that all the people in the neighborhood ran away from until someone finally shot and killed it. After talking about the dream on several occasions, her mother learned that Sue had once wet her pants at school and her teacher and classmates had made fun of her. This mother found that even though she assured her daughter that the incident would surely never happen again, the nightmare continued. Finally, the mother wrote a note to the teacher explaining that her daughter had been experiencing a bladder problem and should be given permission to leave the room at any time to go to the bathroom. Although Sue never needed to use the bathroom privilege, knowing she could if she wanted to put her in control of her fear and ended her nightmare.

When used positively and constructively, nightmares—those dreaded night chillers—can actually teach your children how to confront, understand, and resolve their fears. So when you hear a cry from the dark, comfort your children but don't worry. Consider it no more than another developmental milestone that's giving your children a better understanding of the world and their place in it.

BIBLIOTHERAPY

Alex Fitzgerald's Cure for Nightmares
Kathleen Krull (Little, Brown, 1990)

I had a Bad Dream: A Book About Nightmares
Linda Hayward (Golden Book, 1985)

Jessica and the Wolf: A Story for Children Who Have Bad Dreams
Ted Lobby (Magination Press, 1990)

The Berenstain Bears and the Bad Dream
Stan and Jan Berenstain (Random House, 1988)

PART III
Bedtime Problems

We all have experienced bedtime problems. Some nights we can't sleep; some mornings we can't wake up easily, and there certainly are days when we feel extremely tired. When we suffer these problems, we can generally pass them off as annoying but short-lived. For some people, however, bedtime problems fall into the category of sleep disorders and can't be so easily pushed aside. They are problems that chronically interfere with refreshing sleep. If we don't recognize their symptoms in our children, it's quite easy to mistake them for the other bedtime difficulties discussed earlier. We may think they're caused by bedtime resistance which assumes the child has control over the problem and needs clear-cut bedtime limits to remedy it. Or, we may assume the restlessness that accompanies some of these disorders is caused by bedtime fears which send us scurrying for remedies that offer psychological comfort. Unfortunately, neither limits nor comfort will cure these sleep problems.

The following chapters give you the information you need to recognize the sleep disorders of sleepwalking, night terrors, insomnia, apnea, and narcolepsy. Although you usually can't do much to cure these sleep problems, this section of *Winning Bedtime Battles* will give you what you need to know to recognize, treat, and cope with these five most common disorders.

CHAPTER 9

Sleepwalking

In the movies, the sleepwalker holds his arms out straight in front and walks as if drawn by a magnet, with stiff but steady legs toward a definite goal. Because this image does not at all resemble what sleepwalkers really look and act like, parents such as Jane and Ralph Cannon are often shocked when they first find their children sleepwalking.

The Cannons' son, Ben, has been sleepwalking about twice a month for the past year. His nighttime adventures began quite typically after a high fever at the age of six. Sometimes Ben sleepwalks without actually getting out of bed. He sits up abruptly in his bed for fifteen to thirty seconds and then lies down and goes back to sleep. Neither Ben nor his parents know how often he does this because it's such a quick, quiet, and undisturbing form of sleepwalking. But when Ben ventures out of his bed, his parents worry that he's experiencing some kind of mental instability.

It can be unnerving for parents to watch their sleepwalking children—they act so distant and look so unlike themselves. The facial expression is blank; the eyes are wide open and glassy. Their gaze is undirected and their vision is unfocused. The gait of their walk is unsteady and swaying, and although they appear clumsy and uncoordinated, they are able to maneuver themselves around obstacles and perform simple and sometimes repetitive acts like opening and closing drawers, getting food and eating, and going to the bathroom. Most episodes last just a few minutes but some continue for more than a half hour and the sleepwalker remembers nothing about them in the morning.

Jane Cannon remembers being horrified the first night she realized her seven-year-old son Ben was sleepwalking. She found him at eleven o'clock taking all his clothes out of his dresser drawers and placing them in piles on the floor. When she asked him what he was doing, he mumbled incoherently. When she called his name from the doorway, he ignored her and continued at his task. It was when Jane tried to get Ben to stand up and go back to bed that she saw his glassy, unfocused eyes and knew he wasn't really awake. Jane tried to wake Ben but he didn't respond. So she carried him back to bed, tucked him in, and watched as he immediately closed his eyes and returned to a peaceful sleep. "It scared me to see Ben so deliberately emptying out his dresser," Jane recalls, "while he wasn't even aware that I was in the room. The next morning Ben didn't remember anything about the incident so I called our pediatrician. She said Ben apparently had been sleepwalking and then explained that episodes like Ben's were not so unusual and were nothing to worry about. But I still sometimes feel that there must be something wrong with Ben that causes him to do this."

Jane's pediatrician was right. Childhood sleepwalking is not an abnormal occurrence and in the majority of cases it is not a sign of any deep-seated psychological or physical problem. But it is something that is understandably disturbing to parents and shouldn't be completely ignored. Knowing the facts and the causes of sleepwalking and the typical progression of the sleepwalker's activities should ease your mind and help you find ways to keep your nightwanderer safe from harm.

THE FACTS

Sleepwalking has been the subject of many extensive research studies. From these we know a great deal about this occurrence which is technically called somnambulism. We know that in children sleepwalking is usually a benign problem that is eventually outgrown. It is a part of maturation that at least once affects fifteen percent of all children ages five to twelve. If the first occurrence appears before age ten, it is usually outgrown before age fifteen. Only about two percent continue to sleepwalk as adults. We also know that sleepwalking tends to occur one to three hours after falling asleep and that sleepwalkers do not remember anything about their nighttime jaunts. (This information should assure you that if you find your child playing in her room at four in the morning and the next day she remembers the incident, you most likely have a child who simply couldn't sleep rather than one who is a sleepwalker.)

The development of sleepwalking is seemingly linked to genetic factors. As many as eighty percent of the families of those who sleepwalk include one or more other family members who were also sleepwalkers.[1] Also, when a parent has a history of sleepwalking, the chances of a child doing so are six times as great as when neither parent sleepwalked.[2] And although not clearly isolated as genetic factors, it is interesting to note that sleepwalkers are predominantly male; twenty-three percent are also bedwetters, and ten percent also suffer night terrors (see Chapter Ten).[3] It is of no small coincidence then that Ben Cannon is a seven-year-old who is a chronic bedwetter and who has an uncle who was also a sleepwalker as a child.

THE CAUSES

Sleepwalking occurs as a child starts to make the transition from a deep-sleep state (stage 3) to the lighter-sleep dream state of rapid eye movement (REM). The fact that sleepwalking happens while the sleeper is not yet dreaming negates the age-old belief that a sleepwalker is acting out a dream. When researchers learned that this theory was invalid, they of course wanted to know what else could cause it. Although exact reasons are still difficult to pinpoint, researchers do know that the causes of sleepwalking vary according to the sleepers' age.

In adults, sleepwalking is likely to be symptomatic of a psychological or medical disorder. Although adults who sleepwalk are often predisposed to the disorder through genetic or maturational factors, episodes are most likely to occur and to increase in frequency when the adult is feeling highly stressed or is on certain medications that are known to disrupt the sleep cycle.

In the elderly, sleepwalking is usually an indication of an organic brain syndrome frequently called "nocturnal waking." Because there is a progressive decrease in sleep stages 3 and 4 throughout life, with a virtual absence of stage 4 the onset of sleepwalking episodes similar to those in children or young adults is extremely uncommon in older people.[4] Instead, the most common cause of sleepwalking in the elderly is nocturnal delirium. These episodes often occur in patients with mild or moderate dementia who may function fairly well in the daytime but get up and roam the house at night.

In children, sleepwalking is usually not indicative of serious emotional physical problems, but still its causes are varied and uncertain. Some researchers now believe the problem may actually have biological roots. Scientific evaluation of sleep electroencephalograms (EEG) suggests that sleepwalkers have central nervous system (CNS) immaturity. This theory would explain why, as the child and the central nervous system mature, sleepwalking episodes end spontaneously.

Although sleepwalking seems to have a genetically determined biological base, episodes in children can be sparked by a number of external factors. A high fever, for example, can cause a nocturnal walk because of the way it suppresses sleep stages 3 and 4. This suppression may be followed by a rebound of them, making the sleeper more prone to arousal during this time.[5] Extreme fatigue can also trigger a sleepwalking episode. As previously explained in Chapter One, a biochemical response to sleep loss increases the release of adrenaline and noradrenaline which are stimulating chemicals that fight fatigue and upset sleep patterns; this can extend the amount of time spent in stages 3 and 4. In fact, anything that increases a predisposed child's time in deep sleep will also increase the likelihood of sleepwalking. Such factors include: illness, pain, some medications, excitement, or apprehension.

SOLUTIONS

Sleepwalking is generally not a physical disorder that needs a cure. Also, I have found that in the majority of childhood cases it is not a sign of psychological disturbance so psychotherapy is not an appropriate solution. The only reason I may look for a solution to this problem is that it is dangerous to allow a sleepwalker freedom to roam unsupervised. Although most often sleepwalkers navigate with amazing dexterity, some have been known to harm themselves by banging their heads on doors and walls, bruising their shins on furniture, and even breaking bones by falling down stairs. Others have unlocked doors and ventured outside alone in the dark. Because there is this potential for injury, you do need to take precautions to protect your sleepwalker.

Protective Strategies

If your child is sleepwalking only occasionally and shows no sign of emotional disturbance during each episode, the best course of action is to stop worrying about the act itself and concentrate instead on ways to protect her from the trauma and injury that it can cause. First, when you find your children sleepwalking, don't try to wake them. A person awakened from sleepwalking can become confused, disoriented, and sometimes panicky and aggressive. Tell the child it is bedtime; sometimes the message will register and the child will return to bed. If not, gently steer your night traveler back to her bedroom, help her get back into bed, and stay with her until you're sure she has fallen back to sleep.

The following morning you will of course want to know if your children remember the nighttime experience, but don't alarm them with excessive questioning or a troubled attitude. Children will view their sleepwalking episodes in the same way you do: if you consider them abnormal and frightening, so will your children; if you consider them a normal part of maturation, so will your children.

The most constructive thing you can do to protect a sleepwalking child is to arrange the environment to prevent injury and to signal the start of an episode. To do this, consider the following guidelines:

Safety-Proof the Bedroom

Because you too must sleep during the night, you can't always be standing guard waiting to return your sleepwalker to bed. So to insure that your children won't hurt themselves during a sleep-walking excursion, make the bedroom as danger-free as possible:

- don't leave windows wide open
- lock doors to balconies
- hide sharp-edged toys, scissors, knives, drawing compasses, etc.
- push toys and books to the side and clear away electrical cords so your children won't trip as they walk
- keep sleepwalkers off the top bunk

Block the Doorway

Once the child's bedroom is safety-proofed, you'll need to block the doorway to keep the sleepwalker from meandering into dangerous territory. Don't place a bucket or other small obstacle in the doorway assuming your child will wake when he kicks it; most sleepwalkers maneuver carefully around such door blocks. Don't close and lock the bedroom door because this can be upsetting to the child and it's a fire hazard. Instead, install a safety-gate. A safety-gate at the bedroom door or at the top of stairways will help keep your children in a restricted area without endangering their emotional well-being or safety.

Set Alarms

Although doorway gates keep most children from leaving their rooms, some do manage to climb over or dismantle the gates to continue their walk. For this reason, it's best to rig an alarm system that will wake you (and sometimes even the child) when the room barrier has been penetrated. Any number of creative alarm systems have been rigged by cautious parents with whom I've worked, and certainly after a bit of thought and planning you can devise one that works best for you. Some alarm systems that can successfully catch night strollers are constructed as follows:

- Place a chair piled high with pots and pans on the hallway side of the gate. If the sleepwalker pushes the gate over or climbs over it, the toppling chair will sound the alarm.

- Partially close the bedroom door and put sleighbells or cowbells on the doorknob. If the door is opened, the bells will alert you.
- Place soft infant squeeze toys along side your child's bed. The toys will squeal when they're stepped on and signal the start of a walk.
- Buy the kind of door alarm that is intended to keep toddlers from leaving the house undetected. This same gadget can be installed on the front and back doors of the house as added insurance.

Given what is known about sleepwalking, once you've followed these guidelines you don't need to stay awake all night to keep your child safe. Remember, because sleepwalking occurs as the child is coming out of deep sleep (stage 3), the episodes will likely happen sometime in the first three hours of sleep. Also, it is quite rare for a sleepwalker to venture out of bed more than once a night. (Children who do may need professional help as explained below.) This means then that if your children go to sleep before nine o'clock it is very unlikely they will sleepwalk after midnight, and if they do sleepwalk before this time, their sleep (or yours) won't be disturbed with a recurrence during the remaining night hours.

Professional Help

A neighbor of mine recalls that her younger brother's frequent nighttime adventures disrupted the entire family's sleep for one year. She remembers one night in particular when ten-year-old Rick unlocked the front door while sleepwalking and went to his friend's home two blocks away. He knocked on the door and asked for the sweater he had left there earlier in the day. When his friend's mom opened the door and asked, "Rick, what are you doing here in the middle of the night?" the sound of her voice woke him. Rick stood there for a moment looking very frightened and confused; then in panic he turned and raced down the street toward his home. The neighbor telephoned Rick's mom to tell her what had happened. Before his mother had even hung up the phone, Rick rushed up his porch steps and frantically began knocking on the little diamond-shaped window in the front door.

He punched his hand right through the glass before his mom could open the door. Rick stood there shaking and crying uncontrollably; he didn't remember leaving the house and had no idea why he was outside. After this experience, Rick's parents decided it was time to find out if there was any way to stop this night roaming.

If your child's sleepwalking experiences are frequent (two to three times a night) or intense (accompanied by signs of extreme agitation), or if the sleepwalking puts the child at high-risk for injury, you should seek professional help. In these cases there may be more involved than simple central nervous system maturation; so for the sake of your entire family's sleep needs and peace of mind you should not ignore the problem.

• *Physical Exam*: When you first realize that your child's sleepwalking episodes are occurring more than once a week, explain the situation to your pediatrician and ask for a complete medical checkup. A medical doctor can look for underlying physical reasons known to cause sleepwalking and sleepwalking-like symptoms. Children experiencing psychomotor epileptic seizures, for example, may exhibit behaviors similar to sleepwalking. Fever-related illnesses can also spark sleepwalking episodes, and children with Tourette's syndrome have a significantly higher incidence of sleepwalking episodes. Let your pediatrician do a medical evaluation to rule out such physical factors.

• *Hypnosis*: Psychotherapists who specialize in hypnosis can train many sleepwalking children to awaken the moment their feet hit the floor. One eight-year-old girl, for example, whose mother reported that she was sleepwalking every night between nine and ten o'clock, was able to reduce her nightly walks to only one or two a week after undergoing hypnosis. This child was taught to combine relaxation techniques with practiced imagery to awaken herself fully when her feet touched the floor. Your children too can learn to associate awakening with predetermined triggers such as sitting up in bed, standing up, or touching the door knob.

• *Psychotherapy*: Child psychologists can determine if children's sleepwalking is connected to emotional problems, repressed feelings, or excessive tension. Then, through psychotherapy, sleepwalkers can reduce the frequency of their night wandering by learning to express the things that worry them and to cope with daily pressures.

A typical case of effective psychotherapy which I've recently heard about involved a boy who was sleepwalking about five times a week. During the walk he would cry out and thrash his arms about; his face was often grimaced and he perspired heavily. In therapy, the psychologist learned that the boy came from a very religious family who went to services four times a week at a fundamentalist, conservative church. The clinical data collected indicated that he was a very guilt-ridden, anxious little boy who exhibited a marked preoccupation with religious matters. As the counseling sessions focused on the boy's religious concerns, he was able to verbalize the fear of hell and the devil that had been terrorizing him. Once his parents realized how negatively their son was reacting to religious information he didn't fully understand, they spent much time explaining the church sermons, supporting and encouraging his efforts to understand and follow church doctrine, and offering a more compassionate view of God. A short time later, the sleepwalking episodes became less intense and gradually diminished to sporadic occurrences once or twice a month.

• *Medication*: If a sleepwalking problem persists, a pediatrician or psychiatrist may prescribe medication to reduce the frequency and intensity of the occurrence. Benzodiazepines such as diazepam tend to suppress sleep stages 3 and 4 and therefore can often decrease the number of sleepwalking episodes. However, because it can be unhealthy to alter the sleep cycle of children and because the relapse rate is high when the drugs are withdrawn, treatment with medication should be considered only in severe cases and then used with great caution.

THE CASE OF BEN

Like most children, Ben Cannon's sleepwalking episodes are sporadic and occur less than three times each month. Because he is a bedwetter and has a family history of sleepwalking, it is likely that Ben is going through a developmental stage that he will outgrow. Under these conditions, Ben's parents can stop worrying that he has emotional problems or is suffering from some kind of mental instability.

Jane and Ralph do, however, have two jobs to do while Ben is experiencing sleepwalking episodes: (1) They need to make sure that Ben is safe. They should safety-proof his bedroom, put up safety gates, lock the front and back doors, and rig an alarm system that will alert them if Ben wanders out of the "safe" area. (2) They need to convey to Ben that his sleepwalking is not a big deal. When they talk to Ben about this nighttime activity, they should speak matter-of-factly, and when they talk to friends and relatives about the situation, they should be sure that Ben is out of hearing range if they choose to express concern or annoyance.

Ben too has a job to do to help end his sleepwalking: he has to grow and mature. Most often that's all that really can be done by the child. So if your children sleepwalk occasionally, consider it no more than a part of growing up and give them no more or less than you would give to non-sleepwalking children to help them grow strong, healthy, and with love.

CHAPTER 10
Night Terrors

Imagine you hear your child scream out in the dark. You go to his bedroom to find him running around the room crying in terror. You try to stop him and assure him everything is all right—he's safe. But he pulls away from you, yells out jumbled words, and with eyes wide open but glassy and unfocused, he continues to cry and thrash about wildly. His breathing is rapid and shallow and his heart is pounding. You can't stop him and nothing you do consoles him. Then he returns to bed and sleeps soundly.

This scenario describes a typical night terror. Although this term is meant to describe what the child appears to be experiencing, because he has no recollection of the episode in the morning, it more aptly describes how parents feel when they watch their children act as if possessed by some unseen force. Because night terrors are such disturbing experiences, it's important for you to fully understand what they really are and how you can best manage them.

THE FACTS

Night terrors have several consistent identifying characteristics. They tend to occur in non-dream sleep states about ninety minutes after the child first falls asleep; on occasion they may occur once more three to four hours later. Typical episodes last less than fifteen minutes, but some stretch to a full half hour. It is very difficult

133

to awaken children during a night terror and if awakened they appear disoriented and confused. During the night terror, their eyes are open but they look glassy and unfocused; the children are not aware of anyone else in the room and aggressively resist being comforted or held. In mild cases, they don't cry out but perform repetitive acts like picking at their pillows or thrashing about in their bed. In severe cases the child jumps out of bed and runs actively around the room as if in panic. Most mumble or cry out incoherent phrases, but some may yell out statements such as "He's going to get me!" as if in fear of attack.

About three to four percent of all children experience night terrors. Although the majority of affected children are male and occurrences most commonly peak around age three and disappear by age five, females are not immune and cases have been reported in children from ages six months to thirteen years and beyond.

In most cases, night terrors decrease in frequency and duration as children mature. In one particular study, researchers found that affected children who were younger than three-and-one-half years old experienced approximately one episode per week and these occurrences diminished to only one to two episodes per month when they passed the age of three-and-one-half. On the other hand, these researchers found that when children were over three-and-one-half when they experienced their first night terror, the frequency and duration of the following episodes were more severe than those of younger children.[1]

SOME CAUSES

Most childhood night terrors are *not* caused by psychological trauma. In fact, children experiencing night terrors are consistently found to be perfectly normal. They show no signs of abnormal behavior, abnormal psychological profiles, or abnormal brain activity as recorded on electroencephalograms. In addition, personality and behavioral tests have not been able to isolate a particular "type" of child who is likely to be afflicted by these night frights. In apparent psychological and physical ways, children who suffer through night terrors are no different from other children. Although for these reasons it is difficult to pinpoint what causes night terrors, it's known that genetic, biological, and external trauma factors do influence their occurrence.

Genetic Factors

Like sleepwalking, night terrors run in families. Although it's not fully understood how genetic programming dictates which families will be prone to these sleep disorders, research studies and clinical data show a strong relationship. It has been reported that about eighty to ninety percent of the children who experience night terrors have a close relative who has also encountered the problem. Further supporting the genetic theory, it's interesting to note that the likelihood of identical twins both experiencing night terrors has been found to be six times greater than it is for fraternal (non-identical) twins. If you or your spouse, or your brother or sister, or parents endured the problem of night terrors as a child, it is not at all surprising that your child now wakes and screams out in the night.

Biological Factors

Whether the cause of your child's night terrors is genetic or not, the actual occurrence is most likely related to an immaturity of the central nervous system. Similar to sleepwalking episodes, night terrors tend to occur as a person moves from deep sleep to REM sleep. In children, pre-REM sleep is much deeper and harder to penetrate than in adults. It is in this stage that we carry our sleeping children from the car into the house, change them into pajamas, bring them to the bathroom, and tuck them into bed without ever awakening them. As some children move out of their sound sleep into REM sleep, they react with abrupt and incomplete arousal. For reasons not yet fully known, the struggle to move into the next stage is a terrifying experience for some children. As the child's central nervous system matures, the difficulty resolves itself. This explains why, because adults do not sleep as soundly and do not have such difficulty waking from a deep sleep, they only rarely experience night terrors.

External Factors

Children prone to night terrors by genetic and/or biological factors often experience episodes that are clearly triggered by external fac-

tors. Some children have more night terrors when they are extremely tired. Fatigue disrupts the sleep cycle by pushing the body
to produce adrenalines to keep it going. These body chemicals reduce the amount of time spent in deep sleep states, but then the
body reacts with a rebound of excess time in deep sleep and so
night terrors become more prevalent in children inclined to them.
For example, four-year-old Steve experienced his first night terror
when he was two. In the following two years, he had only two more
episodes. But in the last three months, he has awakened with night
terrors two to three nights every week. Looking for a reason for
this sudden onset of frequent night terrors, Steve's mother explained to me that shortly before this time, his dad took a new job
on the night shift; now he was no longer home to tuck his son into
bed as he had always done since Steve was born. Steve didn't like
this change and so he decided that he would wait for his father to
come home. No matter how carefully his mom explained why he
couldn't stay awake until one o'clock in the morning, Steve per-
sisted in his nightly vigil. He would sit up straight in his bed and
hold his eyes open trying to pass the hours. Although Steve would
always fall asleep before his dad came home, he was losing several
hours of needed sleep each night. He became irritable and difficult
to manage in the day and soon the night terrors began. I was sure
that until Steve resumed a predictable and sufficient sleep schedule, the night terrors would continue.

Another known trigger is emotional trauma. A family divorce,
the birth of a sibling, or even the start of a new school year, could
produce stress symptoms that upset a child's sleep and prompt a
bout of night terrors. When I asked Steve's mother to tell me more
about her husband's new job, it became apparent that she, too,
was unhappy about the job change and the new work schedule. In
fact, she admitted that it had become a source of argument and
marital tension. Adding this fact to Steve's loss of sleep, it was
clear that fatigue and tension together were causing Steve to cry
out in the night.

Physical traumas, too, have been known to increase the frequency and duration of night terrors. High fevers, for example, are
known to upset sleep cycles and bring on episodes of sleepwalking

or night terrors. Pain from ear infections, surgery, or any other physical ailment can also spark night terrors.

SOLUTIONS

Before you can decide how to manage your child's nighttime problem, take time to confirm that it is indeed caused by night terrors. It is quite easy to confuse night terrors with nightmares. When children experience their first night terror, most parents assume the crying and thrashing is caused by a bad dream and so they try to calm and assure their children. How confusing and frustrating to find that soothing words and actions can't stop the rampage. The chart on the following page will help you decide if your child's night crying is caused by night terrors or nightmares.

The wild thrashing and distant look characteristic of night terrors may also be confused with symptoms of epilepsy or, less commonly, hypoglycemia. Both cause children to cry out at night in a heavy sweat, thrash about in their beds, and seem distant and unreachable. Again, the chart below will help you determine the cause of the disruption, but if you have any doubts, be sure to ask your pediatrician to help you diagnose the exact cause of your child's night wakings.

Moderate-Case Solutions
Once you have determined that your child's nighttime problem is caused by night terrors, track how often the episodes occur. If your children experience night terrors almost nightly for two weeks or are twelve years of age or older, their case should be considered "severe" and may require professional help as explained on page 139. However, if your children have not yet reached adolescence and they have night terrors only once or twice a week, they are experiencing moderate night terrors that will most likely go away in time. In the meantime there are several do-and-don't guidelines you should follow to make sure that in the midst of a night terror your children don't injure themselves and that you don't overreact or show excessive concern that will cause them undue worry.

During the Night Terror:
• *Don't* try to awaken or restrain your child. It's true that you can

NIGHT TERRORS	NIGHTMARES
• child often has a family history of night terrors	• child has no family history of night terrors
• normal electroencephelogram	• normal electroencephelogram
• episode usually occurs within ninety minutes of falling asleep	• usually occurs in early morning hours
• has no plot or storyline; child seems to envision one image	• has a storyline
• child appears terrified	• child is moderately fearful
• child returns to sleep easily	• child has difficulty returning to sleep
• child does not recall the incident in the morning	• child remembers the nightmare in the morning
• child has panicky scream upon awakening	• child has no panicky scream upon awakening
• child is not comforted by parental presence and may push away if parent tries to hug or hold	• child is comforted by parental presence
• wild thrashing movements and/or repetitive actions like picking at the pillow	• little or no movement and no repetitive action

often wake children from a nightmare by calling their name, and once awake they calm down. But if you try to awaken children experiencing night terrors, they are likely to become more terrified and confused. Children who have been awakened report a nameless feeling of dread and sometimes a feeling of suffocation as if something heavy were on their chest. As difficult as it is to sit idly by when your child looks so terrified, don't try to stop a night terror—let it run its course.

• *Don't* try to hug or hold children experiencing night terrors. It's quite natural to want to give your children comfort and a sense of safety when they appear so afraid, but in their frenzy they can

NOCTURNAL EPILEPTIC ATTACK
• child has no family history of night terrors; may have family history of seizures
• abnormal electroencephelogram
• occurs late in night toward morning *and* in daytime
• no story or image
• child shows no signs of fear
• child returns to sleep easily
• child can recall the seizure episode in the morning
• child does not scream upon awakening
• child is usually comforted by parental presence
• body stiffening or jerking movements

become aggressively hostile to anyone who comes too near. They'll push you away and sometimes run in fear as if you were their attacker.

• *Do* stay with your children during a night terror. Although there's little you can do to ease the attack, you should sit nearby for safety reasons. You can run interference if your children try to race out the door or flail their arms dangerously close to the bedside lamp or the wall. Clear clutter from the floor so they won't trip and fall. Stay throughout the episode so you can comfort them if they should wake and tuck them back into bed when it's over.

• *Do* remain calm. Yelling to your child to stop it, calling frantically to your spouse, or adding your own pacing and crying to the scene will do nothing to help your children—they can't see or hear you and won't remember a thing in the morning. So try to stay calm.

After the Night Terror:

• *Do* help your children return to peaceful sleep. If your children wake during the night terror, they will be confused and disoriented. Help them settle back to sleep and stay at the bedside to give them a sense of security. If they don't wake, they may lie down on the floor when the night terror is over. When you see that they are calm and ready to slip into the next sleep stage, guide them back to their bed. If they have been perspiring, dry their face and cover them with a blanket.

• *Do* tell them in the morning that sometimes children call out to their parents during sleep because they are afraid but then don't remember doing that when they wake up. Tell you children that they have done this and that it's nothing to worry about. Assure them that if they have any nighttime fears or problems you'll always be nearby.

• *Don't* interrogate. When night terrors first begin, you'll of course want to know if your children remember the incident, but don't ask too many questions or describe the scene in graphic details.

• *Don't* become overly concerned. There's no doubt that watching night terrors is a difficult experience for parents. However, because occasional occurrences are not signs of serious abnormalities and because children don't appear to be negatively affected by night terrors, don't scare your children with your own worries.

• *Don't* stay awake all night waiting for an episode. The first night terror occurrence usually happens within ninety minutes of falling asleep. If your children go to bed at eight P.M. they'll probably wake with night terrors before ten-thirty, so you can go to sleep at eleven without further worry. If your children do wake with night terrors, it is possible but unlikely that they will experience another one within the next three or four hours. Don't stay up waiting for one to occur; it's a rare happening and you'll know by the screams if your child needs you.

• *Don't* create bad sleep habits by taking your children into your bed or by sleeping with them in their bed. This remedy may make *you* feel better, but it has no effect on night terrors. It won't reduce their frequency or the intensity of fear children display while experiencing them. You will, however, start a bad habit that will then cause a number of other bedtime problems (as explained in Part One) that will further disrupt your child's sleep.

Severe-case Solutions

Less than one percent of children who experience night terrors need professional help. But when night terrors disrupt the entire household because they are so intense and frequent, or when they persist into adolescence, professionally-managed techniques such as awakening, psychotherapy, hypnosis, or medication may be used to alter the disruptive sleep pattern and give children and their families restful sleep.

• *Awakening*: A new behavioral technique, developed by Bryan Lask, a psychiatrist at London's Great Ormond Street Hospital for Sick Children, offers new help to children who experience frequent bouts of night terrors. Lask worked with nineteen children between the ages of five and thirteen who had suffered night terrors four or five times a week for an average of eight months. Parents were asked to watch their child for five consecutive nights and find out what time the night terror usually developed. They were then asked to wake their child ten to fifteen minutes before the terror was expected to occur or when the child became obviously restless.

In all these cases, the terrors stopped within a week of starting treatment. In three cases, the problem returned again four to seven weeks later but stopped completely after another week of interruption treatment. All nineteen children were still free of night terrors one year later. Lask believes terrors are caused by a faulty deep sleep phase and so when the disturbed pattern is interrupted, the child reverts to a normal sleep pattern.[2]

• *Psychotherapy*: Intense and persistent night terrors can be a sign of extreme tension. So some children, especially older ones, find relief through expressive psychotherapy. If a child feels great stress during the day, but is unable to talk about the problem or can't find a way to deal with the source of the tension, it's possible for the nightly terrors to serve as a form of physical expression and release. A psychotherapist can help children in this circumstance dig deep to identify the cause of the stress, talk about their feelings, and practice stress management and reduction techniques that will reduce the body's need to vent anxiety through night terrors.

Hypnosis

Hypnosis has been known to successfully end persistent night terrors. A recent study out of Chicago detailed the use of this technique with a ten-year-old boy, Don, who had been having night terrors about twice a week since he was four-years-old (one year after his parents divorced). Six months after the night terrors began, Don watched a horror movie about werewolves and his night terrors then focused on images of himself changing into a werewolf. Six years later, Don's mother sought professional help.

Through hypnosis Don was able to move quickly into a deep trance state. The induction consisted of the finger-lowering technique in which the middle two fingers were raised. They were then slowly lowered as he was asked to watch his fingers as they "go to sleep." After completion of the induction, he was given an explanation of the nature of sleep, stage by stage. The regularity and continual movement of the cycles of sleep were emphasized. He was also given direct suggestions for not dropping too quickly into an extremely deep stage of sleep. A follow-up session was planned and took place one week later. In the interim, Don had one night terror of comparatively and relatively low intensity. The suggestions for dropping off to sleep gradually and having rotating cycles of sleep were reinforced in the second session. Two years later, his mother reported that her son had not had a single recurrence. She said Don seemed happier and less plagued by the family problems and that he was able to watch scary moves which prior to treatment triggered night terrors.[3]

Medication

Medication such as prescribed doses of benzoidiazepine or imipramine at bedtime can suppress deep sleep stages and thus decrease the frequency of night terrors. However, medication should be used only as a last resort. It does not usually solve the problem because once medication is withdrawn the night terrors tend to return (sometimes with increased frequency and intensity). There also is little research data on the long-term effects of suppressed sleep cycles during childhood.

If you find your child's night terrors are intense and persistent, seek professional help. In the Epilogue you'll find a resource number that will help you locate a sleep disorder clinic in your area.

PREVENTION

If your child is prone to night terrors, you may prevent some episodes from occurring by making sure he or she is not overly tired or stressed.

Avoiding Fatigue

Very tired children spend more time in deep sleep states; extending the time spent in "night-terror territory" increases their likelihood. So if your children are prone to night terrors, you can reduce the frequency of episodes by carefully monitoring their sleep habits. Afternoon naps or rest periods are especially effective strategies for keeping children from becoming overtired. Midday quiet time is generally easy to manage on uneventful days, but it is precisely when it becomes difficult to squeeze into busy days that it is most important. Night terrors are known to frequently occur during vacation, holiday seasons, and other very active times. So when you know your child is going to be tired, fight off night terrors by scheduling a nap or rest period.

You can also keep your children from becoming overtired. This helps train your child's body to work on a schedule that fulfills all sleep needs and keeps the sleep cycle in sync. This will not end night terrors, but it will limit their number. Chapters One and Two give detailed information about creating consistent sleep/wake patterns through bedtime routines and established bedtime hours.

Identifying Stress

Like you and me, children live with stress every day of their lives. Most children learn to cope and deal with the things that worry them—whether a poor test grade, a cruel classmate, or a broken toy—by seeking help, explaining their problem, and doing something to resolve the difficulty. But some learn instead to keep their worries and emotions to themselves and hope they go away. These children usually turn the problem into internal stresses like headaches, stomachaches, and nightmares; children already prone to night terrors will find release for their worries in nighttime episodes.

If your child suffers night terrors, look for stressful situations that may be the spark. Spend time just talking about each day's activities in general; often the problem will come out in these casual conversations. But don't go looking for trouble and put worrisome ideas into your child's head. Ask general questions like, "How do you feel about that?" and let your child be the first to broach stressful subjects.

Be careful to show respect and acceptance of your children's feelings. If they say something like, "I'm embarrassed to stand up and talk in front of the class," don't respond with a comment like, "Don't be silly; there's nothing to be embarrassed about." Instead, acknowledge the feeling: "Even many adults feel uncomfortable speaking to groups of people." Then offer help: "Why don't you practice your speech with Dad and me so you feel more confident when you give it to your class." Work to ease the stress, not ignore or dismiss it.

You can also reduce night-terror occurrences by anticipating stressful situations in your child's life. When a new school year starts, give positive and supportive messages; perhaps a summer visit will ease some tension. If you'll be leaving your child with a new sitter, ease into the change slowly and give your child plenty of time to adjust and express any fears or worries. If there is a serious family situation such as a divorce, illness, death, unemployment, etc., talk honestly with your child. If you don't explain what's going on, your children will make up their own scenario which will probably be much worse than the reality of the situation.

Only time will take away the horror of the night from children who suffer night terrors. But while you wait for this period to pass, the information in this chapter can help you understand and accept night terrors.

CHAPTER 11

Other Sleep Disorders

Did you ever have one of those nights when you tossed and turned for hours and just couldn't fall into a sound sleep? This happens to all of us occasionally, but some people suffer from sleep disorders that make a "good night's sleep" chronically unattainable.

Sleep disorders are physical or psychological problems that cause children to lose sleep and suffer excessive daytime sleepiness. Although there are innumerable sleep disorders that fall into this category, this chapter will discuss the three which I feel most commonly cause chronic sleep problems and family distress: insomnia, apnea, and narcolepsy.

These problems not only affect children's sleep, but also have profound effects on their daytime functioning. Think back to when your child was a newborn and your own sleep needs were continuously slighted. Did you feel like jumping into the action at work or in your neighborhood? Did you feel like giving your best effort to long and complex projects? Did you have the energy or desire to be kind, generous, and giving? Most of us felt proud if we just made it through the day without a major calamity.

Children who experience chronic sleep disruption spend their days feeling fatigued and sluggish. They also feel frustrated because they know they're not doing the things they should be doing. Children often become discipline problems because of their inability to follow directions and their irritable moods. They also tend to do poorly in school because they can't concentrate and they lack motivation. If the sleep problem persists, affected children often get caught in a vicious cycle: their daily functioning level is low → parents and teachers voice their disappointment and even anger → the child develops a low sense of self-esteem and personal motivation.

If you think your children suffer from one of the following sleep disorders, you should not wait for them to outgrow it (sometimes they won't). Start your search for a cure by finding the cause of the problem, and then try the at-home remedies suggested in this chapter or seek professional help when recommended.

INSOMNIA

Total insomnia, meaning no sleep at all over an extended period of time, is a very rare occurrence. More commonly, insomnia means continuous "poor" sleep which entails trouble falling asleep, staying asleep, or falling back to sleep in the middle of the night. If your children regularly take longer than thirty minutes to fall asleep or if they wake in the middle of the night and can't go back to sleep within thirty minutes, they may indeed be suffering from insomnia.

As you look for a cure for this problem, it's important to understand that insomnia is not a disease; it is a symptom of some other problem. The cure depends entirely on finding the reason for the sleep difficulty and working to resolve that underlying dilemma.

Sleep Log
In this chapter, I've detailed the signs and symptoms and appropriate remedies for five common causes of childhood insomnia. Read through them all and then pick the one that seems most likely to be affecting your child. Then before you try the suggested remedies, prepare a sleep log. In this log, record the amount of time it presently takes your children to fall asleep each night and note how often they wake during the night and how long it takes them to get back to sleep. Once you begin implementing the suggested remedies, note this same sleep information

every night. If you see no improvement in sleep time after two weeks of treatment, you probably have not found the correct cause. Choose another and continue your sleep-log recordings. If none of the at-home remedies improve the quality and length of your child's sleep, and the insomnia has been present for more than eight weeks, your child may need professional help to pinpoint the source of the sleeplessness and to overcome the problem. (See page 57 for a referral number.)

Roots and Remedies

• *Wrong Bedtime*: Your children may lie awake for more than thirty minutes because they simply aren't tired. Although most children need a fairly standard number of sleep hours each night (as explained on page 11), some need less sleep than the "average."

Six-year-old Lori, for example, baffled her parents with her late night hours. "I put Lori to bed at eight o'clock every night," says her mom, "and then go in to check on her at ten before I go to bed. Every night I find her lying in her bed wide awake. I feel so sorry for her because she just can't fall asleep."

After further questioning, Lori's mother told me that when her two older children were six-years-old they always went right to bed at eight and slept soundly until the morning. She also admitted that Lori had no problem getting up at seven in the morning and wasn't at all tired or irritable during the day. Lori's sleep needs were obviously not the same as her brother's and sister's.

To find out if your child's insomnia is caused by an inappropriate bedtime hour, read the information in Chapter One. It explains how to determine and set an individually correct bedtime hour (page 11), and how to judge your child's internal clock ("circadian rhythm" page 18). Once you consider this sleep information in view of your child's needs, keep track of nightly progress in your sleep log.

Lori's parents kept her getting-ready-for-bed time at eight o'clock, but they told her she was free to play in her room until her new ten o'clock bedtime. Lori continued her usual habit of falling asleep around ten-thirty every night and continued to wake easily and happily by seven each morning. Although Lori's sleep time never actually changed, her "insomnia" ended when her parents changed their attitude about children's sleep requirements. There was no more worry about a sleep disorder as soon as they accepted that their third child needed only eight-and-a-half hours of sleep each night.

• *Overstimulation*: Some persistent cases of insomnia are caused by a lack of physical and mental readiness for sleep. Children who go to bed still feeling stimulated by play or TV or other activities may lie there for longer than a half hour waiting for the body to calm down. Adults who work a late shift or who come home late from the gym know that even though they'd like to go to bed as soon as they get home, they need time to unwind before sleep will come. Children function in the same way.

Carla Mitchell worried that her son wasn't getting enough sleep since she began working late. Although she wasn't happy about leaving him at the baby-sitter's until eight-thirty each night, Carla felt less guilty knowing she could get him home and in bed by nine. But every night, Tyler would lie awake in bed until after ten. Tyler wasn't staying up late because he wasn't tired; he was quite sluggish and irritable during the day. But his mother didn't realize that her son couldn't jump from the baby-sitter's house to his bed and then to sleep. He needed a slower and calmer transition period.

If your children generally jumpstart into bed, establish a calming bedtime ritual that will ease them more slowly into a sleepy frame of mind. (Review Chapter One page 9 for a complete explanation of the purpose and process of calming bedtime rituals.)

To help Tyler unwind on a tight schedule, Carla changed her own coming-home habits. In the past, when they arrived home Carla sent Tyler immediately to his room to get into his PJs while she went to the bathroom to wash and change. She would yell "Good night" while she was reading the mail and listening to messages on the answering machine. Then after throwing in a load of laundry, she'd pop her head into Tyler's room to make sure he was securely tucked in. Carla now goes into Tyler's room as soon as he's dressed for bed. She sits on the bed and holds his hands; she talks about her day and asks Tyler about his. She reads him a story and kisses him good night. This ritual takes only fifteen minutes, but it's calming and comforting, and that's what Tyler needs to fall asleep before ten o'clock.

• *Stress*: We've all experienced the occasional bad night's sleep when we're under stress. Marital tension, job pressures, money concerns can all keep us awake for hours. Children too may have trouble falling asleep because they are worried about something. Childhood is full of stress: school stress, peer stress, parental stress, etc., are all a part of children's lives. The occasional stress-related insomnia is perfectly normal and no cause for concern. But if you find that your children continually lose sleep because they're worrying about something, then it's time to do something about it.

Luann Mearns became very concerned when she found her seven-year-old daughter, Kim, wide awake each night around midnight. "When I'd ask her what was the matter, she'd say, 'Nothing, I just can't sleep.' But then as I'd start to leave her room she'd always call me back to ask me a question that was on her mind." Kim's questions included queries like, "Where will I live if you and Daddy die?" And, "What's an orphan?" And, "How long can you live without food?" Kim had obviously become a chronic late-night worrier.

Most late-night worriers are daytime worriers as well. If your children are often concerned or anxious about things like school, sports, personal appearance, and friendships, then it is possible that their insomnia is caused by stress. If stress is the cause, more communication between the two of you is part of the cure.

One day after school, Kim asked her mother if children are allowed to live in their own house if their parents run away. Kim's daytime and nighttime worries had become clearly focused on a fear of being "orphaned." Although her mother repeatedly assured her she was not going to leave her, Kim still seemed worried. So Luann took this opportunity to dig deeper for the root of Kim's questions. She pressed her daughter to explain why she thought a parent would "run away." In a sudden burst of honesty, Kim told her mother about a story she had heard on a TV news show. It was about a two-year-old girl who had been found near death in a run-down tenement. The child had apparently been abandoned by her parents who had "run away." Getting the story and her fears out in the open helped Kim put the situation in perspective. It also gave Luann something concrete to talk about and offer protection against. From that night onward, Kim was asleep before midnight.

Sometimes, even after the cause of stress is uncovered, children need help learning to relax and cope with their concerns And when the cause can't be pinpointed, it's especially important that children learn how to take their mind off troubling thoughts. In Chapter Five there is a detailed discussion of coping skills that help children deal with their nighttime worries through relaxation techniques. The chapter explains how strategies such as muscle massage and deep breathing can ease the tense muscles and rapid breathing that often accompany stress. It details how positive self-statement can be used to help children reassure themselves when their parents are sleeping and unavailable to give comfort. And the chapter also gives an example of how positive imagery can be used to focus a child's thoughts on happy and secure occasions rather than the fearful ones that keep sleep away.

If you think your child's insomnia is caused by stress, read over Chapter Five and keep a sleep log. Record the wakeful hours before and then after using relaxation techniques. If stress is the cause, your log will show gradual improvement each night.

• *Sleep Habits*: Do you need a blanket or sheet pulled up to your neck to sleep soundly even during a heat wave? Do you need to sleep on the right side of the bed or with one particular pillow to fall asleep easily? If you do, then you can understand how certain sleep-related habits can cause sleep problems when the habit is interrupted. Children too may lie awake for hours unable to sleep because they've developed poor sleep habits. Their insomnia cannot be relieved until they learn more appropriate sleep associations.

The sleep habit that most commonly causes insomnia is the need to be "put" to sleep. As Chapter One explains, we sometimes teach our children to need us nearby in order to fall asleep. We sit by their bedsides until they doze off, or we bring them to our own beds. We may allow them to fall asleep watching TV on the living room couch or to play until they drop on the floor. Unfortunately, when these habits can't be practiced they can cause insomnia. Sometimes, the going-to-sleep habit can't be practiced because the parent is out for the evening, or the children are away visiting at a friend or relative's house, or they wake in the middle of the night and can't reestablish the original going-to-sleep habit by themselves. Chapter One tells you how to use consistent bedtime rituals and a set bedtime hour to teach your children new sleep habits that will enable them to drop off without inappropriate sleep crutches. Once they learn to do this, their insomnia will vanish.

General Guidelines

While you look for the cause of your child's insomnia, there are some general guidelines you should follow to ease the problem. Remember that the most frustrating thing about not being able to fall asleep is thinking about not being able to fall asleep. By focusing so intently on the fact that they're not sleeping, your children add stress to the nighttime problem and further prolong the insomnia. A technique called stimulus control can help break this cycle of chasing away sleep by worrying about not sleeping. Tell your children that if they aren't asleep in thirty minutes, they can and should get out of bed and do something to take their mind off the sleep problem. Encourage them to read, play a quiet game, or listen to the radio. (Don't let them turn on the TV to pass the time or call you to stay with them because these "solutions" promote bad sleep habits that will further complicate the nighttime hours.) After ten or fifteen minutes, your children should return to bed and try once again to fall asleep. If sleep still won't come within thirty minutes, let your children repeat the procedure.

While you're helping your child overcome nightly sleeplessness, be sure you don't inadvertently sabotage your efforts. Don't use the bedroom as a place for punishment during the day because being banished there makes children associate this room with negative feelings and thoughts. This can make it more difficult for an insomniac child to relax and enjoy the comfort of drifting off to sleep. You can remove another obstacle to peaceful sleep by limiting your children's caffeine intake. While you're trying to end this sleep problem, restrict your children's intake of colas and chocolate. This will physically prepare their bodies for sleep.

If your children are losing sleep to insomnia, be sure to keep track of their sleep patterns in your log. When you've zeroed in on the correct cause of the insomnia and practiced the suggested remedies consistently you should see improvement within three weeks.

Professional Help

If you can not find the cause for your children's insomnia or if the remedies suggested in this chapter don't improve their sleep, you should seek professional help. Sometimes insomnia strikes children who are hyperactive and suffer from Attention Deficit Disorder (ADD). Other times insomnia can be a child's way of signaling for help for post-traumatic stress. It can also be a symptom of childhood depression. Each of these problems needs professional attention. See the resource listed in the Epilogue to find a sleep disorder center in your area where your child can receive professional help for insomnia.

APNEA

Apnea is a breathing pause of more than ten seconds that occurs repeatedly during sleep. Apnea disrupts sleep because each time it occurs the body is deprived of oxygen and the sleeper partially wakes in an effort to resume breathing. In severe cases, sleep clinicians have recorded as high as 319 episodes of apnea during seven hours of sleep. This repeated awakening disrupts the sleep cycle and causes the child to feel extremely tired during the day.

The Causes

Although some infants and a few rare older children experience breathing pauses caused by an immaturity of the central nervous system, the most common form of apnea, and the one addressed in this chapter, is caused by an obstruction of the upper airway. Usually the obstruction that inhibits the flow of air during sleep is enlarged tonsils/adenoids. Sometimes the obstruction is fatty tissue in the back of the throat more common in overweight children. And, although no genetic link has been positively identified, there seems to be some inborn factor because apnea most often affects males.

The Symptoms

To determine if your child's sleep problem is caused by apnea, be alert for these signs and symptoms:

- repeated and extended breathing pauses during the night
- chronic loud snoring or labored breathing at night
- mouth breathing when asleep
- mouth breathing when awake
- extreme restlessness during sleep
- frequent waking and gasping for breath

In addition, apnea has some side effects which can point to this problem. You'll notice typical signs of sleep deprivation which include chronic difficulty in rising and daytime sleepiness. Your child may also exhibit little self-control and have difficulty concentrating in school (teachers are often the first to notice the signs of a sleep disorder). In addition, you should suspect apnea if your child is overweight and often wakes with a morning headache. There may also be a relationship between bedwetting and apnea because it has been found that the physical exertion used to resume breathing can push urine from the bladder.

The Treatment

If apnea is causing your child sleep problems, there is little you can do at home to stop the breathing pauses in the night. But the condition shouldn't be ignored because chronic sleep deprivation so drastically affects the quality of life and without treatment apnea can be a lifelong problem. Children with the signs and symptoms of apnea should be professionally diagnosed at a sleep lab.

When apnea is confirmed, several forms of treatment may be recommended. Often, removal of enlarged tonsils and adenoids opens the upper airway and alleviates the problem. If the child is overweight, a reduction diet may cure the problem. Or doctors may propose a management technique called CPAP that provides Continuous Positive Airway Pressure through a small tube inserted into the nose at night. This tube regulates the flow of oxygen and eliminates the nocturnal wakings.

Although you can't treat apnea at home, you can be a part of its cure. Knowing what it is, how it negatively affects your child, and how to get help will keep this nighttime problem from turning into a source of misunderstandings, inappropriate discipline remedies, and a lifelong battle with fatigue.

NARCOLEPSY

Imagine how you would feel and function if you had been awake for 72 hours and were asked to do a repetitive and boring task like adding many columns of numbers. This image gives you some idea how people who suffer narcolepsy feel every day. This sleep problem is a serious lifelong disorder of REM sleep which results in a nearly uncontrollable desire to sleep during the day. Although this sleep disorder is often misunderstood and misdiagnosed it is not a rare disease. In the United State alone, by conservative estimate, 250,000 people suffer from narcolepsy but as many as half of all who have it remain undiagnosed.[1] Since its symptoms are often confused with other sleep problems that result in bedtime battles, you should know its causes and symptoms so you can remain alert to the problem in your own children.

The Causes

Narcolepsy is caused by a malfunction of the REM sleep stage. Usually when we first fall asleep, we go into a stage of nonrapid eye movement (NREM) and after about ninety minutes go into the deep-sleep state of rapid eye movement (REM). This order is reversed in people with narcolepsy; they go from wakefulness immediately into REM sleep. These REM episodes can occur suddenly during the day and cause a person to switch from wakefulness to a sleep state almost instantly.

Narcolepsy is known to run in families. Although the pattern of inheritance is not clear, recent research at the Sleep Disorders Research Center Stanford University's School of Medicine suggests a possible genetic cause. It is theorized that antibodies made by a defective gene in the immune system might be contributing to narcolepsy by interfering with unidentified cells or molecules necessary for healthy sleep.[2] Whatever the exact cause, it has been found that relatives of people with narcolepsy are sixty times more likely to have it themselves than are members of the general population.[3] If anyone in your family exhibits the symptoms of narcolepsy described herein, you should be suspicious that this disorder may be at the root of your child's sleep problems.

The Symptoms

The symptoms of narcolepsy begin subtly and mildly. Afflicted children may first exhibit excessive daytime sleepiness even though nighttime sleep is sufficient and uninterrupted. They will then develop an unusual susceptibility to sleep attacks at inappropriate times. Some, for example, fall asleep in the middle of conversations, others while sitting in class, some while riding bicycles, and still others while eating a meal.

At first the sleep episodes may be so brief that the children and their parents are completely unaware that anything unusual has happened. It would not be uncharacteristic, for instance, for a narcoleptic child to doze off several times during a one-hour homework assignment. In one study at Stanford University, people with and without narcolepsy wore sleep-monitoring devices for an hour while they added columns of figures and performed other tasks requiring concentration. The narcolepsy patients complained that the experimenters had reduced the testing time. They skipped over problems and made far more mistakes than the others. They wrote unintelligible sentences that they couldn't interpret afterward or even remember writing. Periodically, they sat motionless. Their eyes remained open but had a glassy look. The sleep records showed that during the hour, they slept for periods ranging from two to ten minutes. Without realizing why, they performed only half as well as the people without narcolepsy.[4]

The symptom of excessive sleepiness may continue for years, bringing ridicule and negative consequences on children who have no understanding or control over the situation. Recently, a seven-year-old boy named Ronny, who was suffering from undiagnosed narcolepsy, was brought to my sleep clinic by his parents. They were angry with their son because, despite the fact that he was always tired during the day, Ronny would not go to sleep at night before nine o'clock. They came to the clinic looking for a way to stop Ronny from taking afternoon naps which they believed were the cause of his bedtime resistance. As proof of the problem, they brought along letters from his teachers which called the boy, "lazy," "unmotivated," and "inattentive." It seemed reasonable to believe that if Ronny would stop taking afternoon naps and would go to sleep earlier at night, the school problem would be resolved. As reasonable as this solution sounds, Ronny's parents didn't realize that this would actually aggravate rather than ease their son's dilemma.

Although narcolepsy most commonly begins in adolescence, a significant number of cases begin early enough to interfere with elementary school performance. This is why you should be alert to these symptoms in children over the age of six:

- complains of excessive sleepiness
- daytime napping in which the child rapidly falls into a sound sleep
- consistently napping while watching TV or riding in the car

Once narcoleptic children reach their teen years, the disorder may progress to more telltale symptoms. They may notice a momentary muscle weakness triggered by strong emotions like laughing or crying. This condition, called cataplexy, may occur in a split-second during which the knees buckle, or the jaw sags, or head droops forward. Some affected teens have as many as four attacks a day. These teens may also begin to have intensely vivid and often frightening hallucinations just as they are falling asleep. Or, they may experience sleep paralysis in which just before or after sleep they feel unable to move or talk despite a strong desire to do so. Because most children do not experience all the symptoms of narcolepsy, it is especially difficult for parents to diagnose the problem without professional help.

The Diagnosis
Excessive daytime sleepiness is characteristic of a number of sleep

disorders so it is not enough evidence to automatically diagnose the problem of narcolepsy. If you suspect that your child may be suffering from narcolepsy, professional diagnosis at a sleep lab is recommended. The major diagnostic test used at most sleep centers is the multiple sleep latency test (MSLT). During the course of this test, patients are given five or six opportunities to sleep at two-hour intervals during the day. Indicators of narcolepsy include falling asleep in less than five minutes and falling immediately into REM sleep. This test is especially useful for screening children whose parents suffer narcolepsy; early detection and treatment might avert some of the negative physical and psychological problems associated with narcolepsy.

The Treatment

Narcolepsy can not be cured. In adults it is most commonly treated with medications that regulate REM sleep and therefore reduce the number of sleep attacks. But because the given medications sometimes have negative side effects and can be addictive, children are generally treated in ways that teach them to reduce the sleepiness through coping strategies. Naps are particularly helpful in dealing with childhood narcolepsy. Short naps of fifteen to thirty minutes scheduled immediately after school are very refreshing. Also, children with narcolepsy need regular sleep habits; going to bed at an appropriate hour each night will help them wake spontaneously and renewed every morning. In addition, children can be taught how to work midday rest periods into their schedules without calling attention to themselves by napping, for example, while sitting on a toilet in the restroom. Children can also be taught how to fight sleep with stimulating activities like rapid blinking, hand flexing, walking, and muscle stretching.

If you would like more information about narcolepsy or would like to join a self-help group, contact the American Narcolepsy Association (ANA), P.O. Box 5846, Stanford, California 94305.

These three sleep disorders do more than interfere with your child's sleep. They can negatively affect each day's simplest achievements and accomplishments. I've noticed that they can also cause children to misjudge their own worth and capabilities.

And in the long run, they take away the joyful quality of life that we all wish for our children. If you suspect that your child is suffering a sleep disorder that can't be remedied at home, call the sleep lab nearest you for a professional evaluation.

Epilogue

The prize for winning bedtime battles is awarded to your children. If you win over your children's bedtime rebellion and bad habits, they gain healthy sleep patterns that give them the energy and motivation they need to give their best effort to each new day. If you win over their bedtime fears, your children gain coping strategies and confidence that will help them confront other fears that threaten to intimidate them in the future. And if you win over the confusion and misunderstandings caused by sleep disorders, your children will gain your support and comfort as well as a realistic understanding of their problem and the knowledge how they can best cure or cope with it.

Although the majority of sleep problems experienced by children ages two through ten can be diagnosed and remedied with the information given in this book, sometimes the problem may be severe or persistent enough to require professional help. If you do not see improvement in your child's sleep habits after one full month of at-home treatment, follow these guidelines:

• See your pediatrician. Ask that your child be given a physical examination to rule out urinary-tract disorders, diabetes, middle-ear infection, or other health problems that may cause or contribute to sleep disturbance.

• If your doctor prescribes medication to ease the problem situation, keep in mind that this is generally a short-term solution that doesn't solve the underlying cause of the sleep problem. Medication can sometimes effectively break the pattern of disturbance and restore a normal sleep pattern, but most often the symptoms return when the medication is withdrawn. Use drug therapy sparingly and only under strict medical supervision.

• If an underlying psychological problem is suspected, ask your pediatrician for a referral to a psychologist, psychiatrist, or family counselor who specializes in childhood sleep problems.

• If the sleep problem continues to persistently interrupt your child's sleep and/or disrupt daily functioning you may find relief in the diagnostic help and treatment recommendations offered at a sleep-disorder clinic. For a list of sleep-disorder centers near you, send a business-size, self-addressed, stamped envelope to: Association of Sleep Disorder Centers, 1610 14th Street N.W., Suite 300, Rochester, Minnesota 55901.

Although I can't diagnose sleep problems by phone or mail, if you find sections of this book to be especially helpful or problematic, please drop me a note. As my work with childhood sleep problems continues, I'm always eager to hear what parents find worthwhile, confusing, or useless. Direct your letters to:

Dr. Charles Schaefer, Director of Better Sleep Center
Division of Psychological Services
Fairleigh Dickinson University
139 Temple Avenue
Hackensack, New Jersey 07601

Notes

1. Bad Bedtime Habits

1. Trish Hall, "The Battle of Bedtime: Children Won," *New York Times*, March 1, 1990, p. C1.
2. Dave Barry, *Dave Barry's Guide to Marriage and/or Sex*. Emmaus, Pennsylvania: Rodale Press, 1987.

2. Bedtime Rebellion

1. Lisa A. Adams and Vaughn Rickert, "Reducing Bedtime Tantrums: Comparison Between Positive Routines and Graduated Extinction," *Pediatrics*, 84:5, November 5, 1989, pp. 756-61.

4. Nightwaking

1. Frederick Seymour, Gay Bayfield, et al., "Management of Night-Waking in Young Children," *Australian Journal of Family Therapy*, 4:4, 1983, pp. 217-23.
2. Seymour, Bayfield, et al.

PART II. INTRODUCTION

1. Thomas W. Draper and Rebecca Smoak James, "Preschool Fears: Longitudinal Sequence and Cohort Changes," *Child Study Journal*, 15:2, February 1985, p. 153.

6. Fear of Things that Go Bump in the Night

1. Maria Mihalik, "Calming the Fears of Children," *Children*, April 1988, p. 36.
2. Lisabeth DiLalla and Malcolm Watson, "Differentiation of Fantasy and Reality: Preschoolers' Reactions to Interruptions in Their Play," *Developmental Psychology*, 24:2, March 1988, p. 286.

3. Nancy Binzen, "'Monsters' Help Keep Children Healthy," *Child's Play*, September 1987, p. 7.

9. Sleepwalking

1. A. Kales, C. Soldatos, E. Bixler, "Hereditary Factors in Sleepwalking and Night Terrors," *British Journal of Psychiatry*, 137, 1980, pp. 111-18.

2. Richard Berlin and Suman Qayyum, "Sleepwalking: Diagnosis and Treatment Through the Life Cycles," *Psychosomatics*, 27:11, November 1986, pp. 755-60.

3. J. Simmonds and H. Parraga, "Prevalence of Sleep Disorders and Sleep Behaviors in Children," *Journal of The American Academy of Child Psychiatry*, 21, 1982, pp. 383-88.

4. A. Kales and J. Kales, "Recent Findings in the Diagnosis and Treatment of Disturbed Sleep," *New England Journal of Medicine*, 290, 1974, pp. 487-99.

5. J. Kales, A. Kales, and C. Soldatos, "Sleepwalking and Night Terrors Related to Febrile Illness," *American Journal of Psychiatry*, 136, 1979, pp. 1214-15.

10. Night Terrors

1. Francis J. DiMario, et al., "The Natural History of Night Terrors," *Clinical Pediatrics*, 26:10, October 1987, pp. 505-11.

2. Geoff Lowe, "Taming Children's Night Terrors," *Psychology Today*, March 1989, pp. 76.

3. Richard Kramer, "The Treatment of Childhood Night Terrors Through the Use of Hypnosis: A Case Study," *The International Journal of Clinical and Experimental Hypnosis*, 37:4, 1989, pp. 283-84.

11. Other Sleep Disorders

1. Lynne Lamberg, *The American Medical Association Guide to Better Sleep*. New York: Random House, 1984, p. 174.

2. "Narcoleptics May Have an Immune Disease," *Science News*, April 27, 1991, p. 271.

3. Lamberg, 174.

4. Lamberg, 183.

Index

Advice for Parents - Fun For Kids

Children's Letters to Santa Claus, Compiled by Bill Adler   hardcover $9.95   (#72196)

Creative Family Projects: Exciting and Practical Activities You Can Do Together by Cynthia MacGregor   paperback $9.95   (#51636)

Cults: What Parents Should Know by Joan Carol Ross, Ed.M. & Michael D. Lange, Ph.D.   paperback $5.95   (#40511)

The Day Care Kit : A Parent's Guide to Finding Quality Child Care by Deborah Spaide   paperback $7.95   (#72031)

Getting Straight A's by Gordon W. Green, Jr., Ph.D.   paperback $9.95   (#40571)

Great Videos For Kids: A Parent's Guide to Choosing the Best by Catherine Cella   paperback $7.95   (#51377)

Grown Up Children, Grown Up Parents: Opening the Door to Healthy Relationships Between Parents and Adult Children by Phyllis Lieber, Gloria S. Murphy, and Annette Merkur Schwartz   hardcover $18.95   (#72243)

Helping Your Child to Learn by Gordon W. Green, Jr., Ph.D.   paperback $9.95   (#51497)

Helping Your Child to Learn Math by Gordon W. Green, Jr., Ph.D.   paperback $10.95   (#51613)

How to be a Pregnant Father by Peter Mayle; illustrated by Arthur Robins   paperback $9.95   (#40399)

How to Solve Your Child's Reading Problems by Ricki Linksman   paperback $12.95   (#51618)

Kids' Book of Baseball: Hitting, Fielding, and the Rules of the Game by Godfrey Jordan   paperback $8.95   (#51620)

Kids' Letters From Camp, Edited by Bill Adler   hardcover $9.95   (#72226)

Kids Pick the Best Videos for Kids by Evan Levine   paperback $9.95   (#51498)

Maybe You Know My Kid: A Parent's Guide to Identifying, Understanding and Helping Your Child With Attention Deficit Hyperactivity Disorder by Mary Fowler   paperback $12.95   (#72209)

Mother Knows Best?: The Truth About Mom's Well Meaning (but not always accurate) Advice by Sue Castle   paperback $8.95   (#51631)

The *Reading Rainbow* Guide to Children's Books by Twila C. Liggett, Ph.D. and Cynthia Mayer Benfield; Introduction by LeVar Burton   paperback $12.95   (#51493)

The Santa Claus Book by Alden Perkes   paperback $14.95   (#40381)

Teaching Your Kids to Care: How to Discover and Develop the Spirit of Charity in Your Children by Deborah Spaide   paperback $9.95   (#51637)

Upside Down Tales: Two books in one-- a classic children's tale, and an alternative, amusing version that sets the record straight!
Hansel & Gretel/The Witch's Story by Sheila Black; Illustrated by Arlene Klemushin   paperback $8.95   (#51520)
Jack & The Beanstalk/The Beanstalk Incident by Tim Paulson; illustrated by Mark Corcoran   paperback $8.95   (#51313)
Little Red Riding Hood/The Wolf's Tale by Della Rowland; Illustrated by Michael Montgomery   paperback $8.95   (#51526)
The Untold Story of Cinderella by Russell Shorto; illustrated by T. Lewis   paperback $8.95   (#51298)

"What's Happening to Me?" by Peter Mayle; illustrated by Arthur Robins   paperback $8.95   (#40312)

"Where Did I Come From?" by Peter Mayle; illustrated by Arthur Robins   paperback $9.95   (#40253)

"Why Am I Going to Hospital?" by Claire Ciliotta & Carole Livingston; illustrated by Dick Wilson   paperback $8.95   (#40568)

"Why Was I Adopted?" by Carole Livingston; illustrated by Arthur Robins   paperback $8.95   (#40400)

Winning Bedtime Battles: How to Help Your Child Develop Good Sleep Habits by Charles E. Schaefer & Theresa Foy DiGeronimo   paperback $9.95   (#51318)